W9-AYS-931

Latino-American History

Independence
for
Latino America

1776–1821

Latino-American History

Latino-American History

Independence for Latino America

1776–1821

by Richard Worth

Mark Overmyer-Velázquez, Ph.D., Consulting Editor

CHELSEA HOUSE
PUBLISHERS
An imprint of Infobase Publishing

COVER *At San Diego in 1759, Father Junípero Serra founded the first mission in California, shown here.*

Independence for Latino America

Copyright ©2007 by Infobase Publishing

For information contact:

Chelsea House
An imprint of Infobase Publishing
132 West 31st Street
New York, NY 10001

Library of Congress Cataloging-in-Publication Data
Worth, Richard.
   Independence for Latino America / Richard Worth.
      p. cm — (Latino American History)
   Includes bibliographical references and index.
   ISBN 0-8160-6441-5
   1. Latino Americans—History—Juvenile literature. 2. Immigrants—United States—History—Juvenile literature. 3. Mexican Americans—Juvenile literature. I. Title. II. Series.
   E184.M5W675 2005
   304.8'73072—dc22
2004014302

Chelsea House books are available at special discounts when purchased in bulk quantities for businesses, associations, institutions, or sales promotions. Please call our Special Sales Department in New York at (212) 967–8800 or (800) 322–8755.

You can find Chelsea House on the World Wide Web at **http://www.chelseahouse.com**

Cover design by Takeshi Takehashi

A Creative Media Applications Production
Interior design: Fabia Wargin & Luis Leon
Editor: Matt Levine
Copy editor: Laurie Lieb

Photo Credits
The Granger Collection, New York, pages: cover, vi, 12, 16, 45, 85, 88, 92, 95; North Wind Picture Archives pages: 8, 31, 36, 39, 40, 78, 81; California Historical Society pages: 20, 24; © Private Collection/Peter Newark American Pictures/The Bridgeman Art Library page: 26; New York Public Library, Astor, Lenox and Tilden Foundations pages: 35, 48, 54, 64, 68; © Bibliotheque Nationale, Paris, France, Lauros/Giraudon/ The Bridgeman Art Library page: 58; Library of Congress page: 70; © Royal Geographical Society, London, UK/The Bridgeman Art Library page: 76

Maps: Created by Ortelius Design

Printed in the United States of America

Bang CMA _____ _____ 10 9 8 7 6 5 4 3 2 1

This book is printed on acid-free paper.

All links and Web addresses were checked and verified to be correct at the time of publication. Because of the dynamic nature of the Web, some addresses and links may have changed since publication and may no longer be valid.

Contents

Preface to the Series

**by Mark Overmyer-Velázquez, Ph.D.,
Consulting Editor**

"With all due respect to Uncle Sam, this [march] shows that Los Angeles has never stopped belonging to Mexico." This statement by Alberto Tinoco, a television reporter in Mexico, refers to the demonstration in support of immigrants that took place in Los Angeles, California, on March 25, 2006. An estimated 1 million people attended this march—mainly Mexicans and other Latinos. But does Los Angeles belong to Mexico? And what was so important that so many people came out to show their support for Latino immigrants?

The *Latino American History* series looks to answer these questions and many others. Los Angeles did belong to Mexico until 1848. At that time, Los Angeles and much of what is now called the American Southwest became part of the United States as a result of the Mexican-American War. Today, the enormous city, like many other places throughout the United States, is home to millions of Latinos.

The immigrant march made perfectly clear that people of Latin American descent have a historical power and presence in the United States. Latino history is central to

OPPOSITE On September 16, 1810, Father Miguel Hidalgo y Costilla issues his *Grito de Dolores* (Cry of Dolores), calling on the Mexican lower classes to rise up against the Spanish government.

the history of the United States. Latinos have been closely connected to most regions in the United States in every era, from the 16th-century Spanish settlements in Florida and California to the contemporary surge of Latino populations in North Carolina, South Carolina, Oklahoma, Minnesota, and Connecticut.

The 2000 U.S. Census made Latinos' importance even plainer. Every 10 years, the government makes a survey of the country's population, called a census. The 2000 survey determined that, for the first time, Latinos outnumbered African Americans as the second-largest nonwhite population.

One of every seven people in the nation identifies himself or herself as Latino. This ethnic group has accounted for about half the growth in the U.S. population since 1990. There are over 41 million people of Latin American and Caribbean origins in the United States. Their presence will have a large impact on the futures of both the United States and Latin America.

Who Is Latino?

The term *Latino* emerged in the 1970s. It refers—somewhat loosely—to people, either male or female, living in the United States who have at least one parent of Latin American descent. The term is often used in contrast to terms such as *Anglo American, African American,* and *Asian American.* Most frequently, *Latino* refers to immigrants (and their descendants) who originally came to the United States from the Spanish-speaking countries of North, Central, and South America, as well as from countries in the Caribbean. This definition usually does not include Brazil, Haiti, and Belize, where the chief language is not Spanish, but does include Puerto Rico, which is a U.S. territory.

The other popular term to describe this population, *Hispanic,* was developed by the U.S. government in the 1970s as a way to categorize people of Latin American descent. However, Latinos consider this label to wrongly identify them more with Spain than with Latin America. In addition, most Latinos first identify with their own national or subnational (state, city, or village) origins. For example, a woman with roots in the Dominican Republic might first identify herself as *una dominicana* and then as a Latina. The word *Latino* causes further confusion when discussing the thousands of non–Spanish-speaking American Indians who have immigrated to the United States from Latin America.

Four main factors over time have determined the presence of Latinos in the United States. They are U.S. military and economic involvement in Latin America, relaxed immigration laws for entry into the United States, population growth in Latin America, and wages that were higher in the United States than in Latin America. These factors have shaped the patterns of migration to the United States since the mid-19th century.

"We Didn't Cross the Border, the Border Crossed Us"   1848

Many Mexicans still call the Mexican-American War from 1846 to 1848 the "North American Invasion." In the first decades of the 19th century, Mexico's economy and military were weak from years of fighting. There had been a war for independence from Spain followed by a series of civil wars among its own people. During the same period, the United States was eager to expand its borders. It looked to Mexico for new land. The war cost Mexico almost half its territory, including what would become the U.S. states of California, Nevada, Arizona, New Mexico, and Texas. Some Mexican citizens left on the U.S. side of the new border proclaimed, "We didn't cross the border, the border crossed us."

The territory that had belonged to Mexico brought new citizens of Mexican background to the United States, as well as enormous mineral and land wealth. Consider the famous gold rush that started in 1848 on former Mexican territory in California. That event and the vast expanse of farmlands and pasture lands once belonging to Mexico were vital to the westward expansion of the United States. Mexicans on the north side of the new border became U.S. citizens and the country's first Latinos. As the West became industrialized and demand for labor grew, it was often migrant Mexican workers who labored in the fields and factories of the prospering economy.

1898   The Spanish-American War, Puerto Rico, and the Harvest of Empire

The term *harvest of empire* refers to the arrival of Latino immigrants in the United States as a direct result of U.S. military involvement in Latin America, starting with Mexico in 1848. The United States created political and economic uncertainty through the use of force and the support of dictatorships in the "garden" of Latin America. Then the United States harvested the resulting millions of homeless and jobless Latinos. The United States's harvest of empire peaked with the 1898 Spanish American War.

The U.S. military freed the island of Puerto Rico from Spanish colonial rule in 1898. The island's residents never would have imagined that they would be colonized yet again, this time by the United States. The island became a U.S. territory. The U.S. president had the power to choose the governor and other high-level administrators. In 1917, Congress made all Puerto Ricans U.S. citizens.

In the 1950s, Puerto Rico suffered economic problems and joblessness. Immigration to the United States rapidly expanded, resulting in the largest movement of Latin Americans to the United States in history. New laws in the 1960s only increased Latin American immigration to the United States.

> **Fast Fact**
>
> American Indians who have migrated to the United States may identify themselves with a small village or perhaps a state of origin. For example, Zapoteco immigrants from the state of Oaxaca, Mexico, have developed Oaxacan hometown associations in Los Angeles and other U.S. cities.

The Hart-Celler Act and Recent Latino Migration

1965

On October 3, 1965, President Lyndon Johnson signed the Hart-Celler Act, introducing a new era of mass immigration. The act made people's work skills and their need to unite with their families the most important elements in deciding who could immigrate to the United States. The new legislation eventually ended a system that used people's countries of origin to decide the number of immigrants who were allowed into the United States. The Hart-Celler Act supposedly put people of all nations on an equal footing to immigrate to the United States. The act created the foundation for today's immigration laws.

Between 1960 and 2000, Latin America's population skyrocketed from 218 million to over 520 million. Political instability in the region, in addition to this growing population, meant increased needs for migration and work. Many people turned to the economic opportunities of the United States as a strategy for survival.

At the same time, in the United States, agricultural, industrial, and domestic employers depended upon the ability to pay immigrant laborers from Latin America lower wages. As a result, Latino labor has almost always been welcomed in the United States, despite the government's repeated attempts to restrict immigration in the past century. The demands of U.S. employers for Latino immigrant labor have always shaped the tone of the immigration debate.

Many Latino Histories

The events of the years 1848, 1898, and 1965 explain how and why Latinos migrated to the United States. However, these events do not

Fast Fact

In 1960, 75 percent of the foreign-born population of the United States came from Europe. Only 14 percent came from Latin America and Asia. As a result of the Hart-Celler Act, by 2000, only 15 percent of immigrants were European and more than 77 percent were Latin American and Asian. This trend promises to continue.

reveal much about what happened once the Latinos arrived. Despite their many shared experiences, Latinos are anything but an easily defined people. Although television and film have tended to portray all Latinos as similar, they come from a wide range of national, ethnic, social, economic, and political backgrounds, which have divided as much as united this growing population. Such backgrounds include "African," "Anglo," "Asian," "Indian," and any combinations of these.

Mexicans started migrating to the United States in the 19th century and Puerto Ricans in the early 20th century. Immigrants from Chile, Argentina, El Salvador, Guatemala, and other South and Central American countries made their way north in large numbers starting in the 1960s. Many of these Latinos were seeking shelter from brutal military dictatorships. Once in the United States, Latinos of all backgrounds have continued to mix with each other and with local populations, forging a whole new set of identities. Latino communities keep and develop their own cultures in new and creative ways in the United States, adding to the rich diversity of the country.

Indeed, Latinos have contributed to U.S. society in other ways besides their investments in the country's economy and labor. In politics, education, sports, and the arts, Latinos are a growing presence. By exploring the origins and development of U.S. Latinos, this series, *Latino American History,* helps us to better understand how our Latin American neighbors to the south have become our Latino neighbors next door. ▣

Introduction

The Spanish encounters with the New World began in 1492, when Christopher Columbus sailed to the New World, as the lands in the Western Hemisphere were then known in Europe. At first, the Spanish took control of islands in the Caribbean Sea from the American Indians.

During the 16th century, the Spanish conquered the Aztec Indians in what is now Mexico and the Inca in present-day Peru. During the conquests, the Spanish discovered that the Indians had collected rich treasures of gold and silver. The Spaniards also found rich silver mines in Mexico and South America. The Spanish enslaved the conquered Indian tribes and forced them to work in the mines. As large shipments of gold and silver were transported back across the Atlantic Ocean, Spain became the wealthiest nation in Europe.

Mexico was called New Spain by the Spanish. From New Spain, the Spanish began to expand their explorations northward. In the 1540s, Francisco Vásquez de Coronado led an expedition to present-day New Mexico, California, and Arizona. The primary motive for Coronado's expedition and the others that followed was the desire for riches. When no treasures were found, the Spanish returned to New Spain.

OPPOSITE Spanish troops attack the Aztecs at the Aztec capital of Tenochtitlán in 1520.

The Spanish came back in the 17th and 18th centuries—this time to establish permanent settlements in the North American Southwest. The Spanish had never given up their dream of finding cities filled with vast treasures like those in Mexico and South America. But just as important was Spain's desire to prevent other nations, such as France and Russia, from occupying California and the Southwest, where they might threaten New Spain.

In addition, the Spanish conquistadores saw themselves as Christian knights. Beginning in the eighth century, Spain had been ruled by Muslim conquerors. Over the next seven centuries, the Christians had gradually pushed back the Muslim armies. Finally, in 1492, the Spanish reconquered all of Spain.

After the retaking of Spain, the conquistadores looked beyond Spain to other lands that might be converted to Christianity. They were convinced that it was their mission to bring the teachings of Christ to people who were not yet Christians.

The pattern of Spanish settlement thus arose from Spain's desire to defend its territory from other nations and the belief that the Spanish had a duty to convert the American Indians to the teachings of Christianity. This pattern was far different from English settlement along the Atlantic coast during the same period. The English were primarily interested in establishing towns and enjoying religious freedom. They were not interested in converting the local Indians to Christianity. The English settlers established communities in the 17th century that grew very large as more settlers came to the Atlantic coast over the next 150 years. By contrast, the Spanish territory that would one day be the U.S. Southwest and California consisted of forts, or presidios, and only a few small towns, like San Francisco, Santa Fe, and San Antonio. The population remained low for many years.

Nevertheless, by the end of the 18th century, the Spanish had named and colonized New Mexico, Arizona, California, and Texas territories that became U.S. states. The settlements at Santa Fe, San Francisco, and San Antonio would grow into large U.S. cities. The Spanish introduced the horse, which transformed the culture of the American Indians on the Western plains. Finally, the Spanish established traditions such as the mission style of architecture that have become part of U.S. culture.

At the beginning of the 19th century, the residents of New Spain began a revolution to achieve their independence from Spain. In 1821 Mexico achieved its own identity as an independent nation and took control of the colonies on the frontier. The success of the independence movement had a large impact on the Spanish colonies in California and along the frontier.

Even as the colonies adjusted to independence from Spain and an independent government in Mexico, they faced a new challenge: U.S. settlers who were migrating westward. These settlers were looking for new places to live within California, Texas, New Mexico, and Arizona. Mexican leaders feared that the new settlers would quickly overwhelm the small Mexican population along the frontier. Soon, U.S. settlers on the frontier would seize these colonies from Mexico, producing a new conflict that helped create the United States as it is today.

The Settlement of California

1

Since the 16th century, the Spanish had conquered an enormous empire that stretched from South America to what is now Mexico and northward to Baja (Lower) California. The area of present-day Mexico and Central America was called New Spain, and it was governed from Mexico City. Russian and British traders began moving from Canada into northern California during the 18th century. To stop this threat to New Spain, the Spanish viceroy, or governor, decided to send an expedition into Alta (Upper) California.

In June 1769, a mule train carrying supplies from Baja California reached the harbor at San Diego. This area had been charted by Spanish explorers two centuries earlier, so the Spanish knew roughly where San Diego was located. Riding at the front of the mule train was a Franciscan priest, Father Junípero Serra.

Miguel José Serra was born in 1713 on the island of Majorca in the Mediterranean. Serra was educated by the Franciscans on the island. Priests in this order, founded

OPPOSITE Father Junípero Serra (center) is shown arriving at San Diego, California, in 1769 as part of Gaspar de Portolá's expedition from New Spain.

by St. Francis of Assisi in the 13th century, were teachers and missionaries. When he was 15, Serra entered Lullian University in Palma, the capital of Majorca. Soon afterward, he decided to join the Franciscan religious order. He was given the name Junípero, after one of St. Francis's companions. After graduating from Lullian University, Father Serra taught in Palma for many years. Then in 1750, at age 36, he decided to become a missionary in the New World.

After arriving on the coast of New Spain, Serra walked to Mexico City, the capital. It was a distance of 260 miles (418 km). Along the way, he was bitten in the leg by an insect that left him permanently crippled. Serra worked at the College of San Francisco in Mexico City. In 1767, he was appointed head of the Spanish missions in Baja California. A mission was a settlement where Christianity was preached for the first time in an area where there were no native priests.

A short time later, Serra was asked to take on a new assignment. The Spanish king, Charles III, had sent a lawyer named José Gálvez as a special envoy to New Spain in 1765. Gálvez was sent to Mexico City to improve the administration and make tax collections more efficient. Meanwhile, Russian traders had crossed from Asia into present-day Alaska, journeying south to northern California. They were trapping seals and otters, whose pelts were widely prized as fur for warm coats. Gálvez decided that the Russian push southward threatened Spanish settlements in Baja California. Therefore, he sent Father Serra to California to found new missions in the name of Spain.

The expedition into California was organized under the direction of Gaspar de Portolá. A Spanish soldier who had served in Europe, he had been named governor of Baja California in 1768. The Spanish expedition includcd about 200 soldiers and some American Indian allies. The soldiers were called leather jackets because they wore leather chest armor to protect themselves from arrows fired by hostile Indians. They also carried muskets and leather shields. Accompanying the soldiers were Father Serra and several other Franciscan priests.

Some members of the expedition traveled by sea. Soldiers were packed aboard two small ships, the *San Carlos* and the *San Antonio*. These ships braved heavy headwinds and rough seas before finally arriving in San Diego. The *San Carlos* lost its way and took 110 days to reach San Diego. By the time the ships arrived, many of the men had died from scurvy. This disease is caused by a lack of vitamin C. A third ship carrying essential supplies was lost at sea.

The Expulsion of the Jesuits

In 1767, two years after sending Gálvez to New Spain, Charles III made another far-reaching decision. For more than 200 years, priests of the Jesuit order had worked in the New World, converting American Indians to Christianity. Since the order's founding in 1540, it had become very powerful throughout Europe, the Far East, and the Western Hemisphere. As a result, European kings in Portugal, France, and finally Spain expelled the Jesuits from their nations and their empires. The Jesuits in New Spain were arrested. In Baja, California governor Gaspar de Portolá rounded up the 16 Jesuits who worked with the Indians. According to historian Ralph Roske, "many of their Indian converts [were] weeping as they departed." Their missionary work was taken over by the Franciscans and the Dominicans, another order of Catholic priests.

Meanwhile, Portolá and Serra led other members of the expedition, including soldiers and local Indians, 350 miles (563 km) overland from Baja to San Diego. As they marched northward, the expedition gradually ran out of supplies. Portolá wrote that "as a result some of the Indians died, and the rest of them deserted from natural necessity." The expedition survived by hunting game and fishing in nearby streams along the route. On July 1, 1769, the expedition reached San Diego.

The First Mission

About two weeks later, Father Serra dedicated the site of the first mission in California. He located the new mission, St. Didacus of Alcala, on a hill with a view of San Diego Bay. The Spanish built a wooden church with a thatched roof and a wooden stockade that was defended by a few leather jackets.

The first mission in California, founded by Father Junípero Serra in San Diego in 1769, is shown in this drawing from the late 19th century.

Much of the Spanish empire in the New World had been created this way. The Spanish saw their role as twofold. One part was conquest. They wanted to control the lands and any gold or silver that might be found there. Indeed, New Spain was an area rich in silver mines that had sent a steady stream of precious metal back to Spain since the 16th century. The Spanish also believed that part of their purpose in conquering the New World was to convert the local American Indians to Christianity. Therefore, priests often accompanied the soldiers. A mission, according to historian Dorothy Krell, was "inexpensive to launch—one or two padres [priests], a handful of soldiers, and a load of supplies—and once established, it soon became self-supporting and later served as the nucleus for permanent settlement."

Many of the missions were laid out in a square. Inside the square was a large plaza. The church was built in one corner of the square. In other parts of the mission were workshops, storerooms, and quarters for the women.

The missionaries provided gifts of clothing, beads, and other trinkets that appealed to the local Indians. Then the missionaries lured the Indians into the mission and put them to work. In return for food and shelter, the Indians were taught how to raise sheep and cattle, grow wheat, and plant grape vines. They also were trained as blacksmiths, weavers, and potters. In a short time, the mission became a self-supporting operation. There was plenty of wheat to make bread, cattle for meat, and cattle hides that were made into leather clothing. The missions grew grapes for making wine and planted orchards to supply pears, peaches, apples, and other fruits. Indeed, the missions often had surplus food that they sent south to New Spain. In return, they purchased furniture, musical instruments for church celebrations, cooking utensils, and other items.

The Indians who lived at the missions were educated by the priests. Generally, they were taught Spanish. As a result, Spanish spread throughout much of California. The Indians were expected to give up their own gods and dedicate themselves to Christianity. Church services were held several times daily, and the Indians were required to attend. Celebrations were held on special feast days throughout the year, giving the Indians a break from the routine of work and prayers.

Some of the Indians lived in villages, or pueblos, near the missions. Generally, the priests appointed Indian alcaldes—town officials—to enforce order in the communities. According to 19th-century historian Guadalupe Vallejo, who grew up in California,

Indian alcaldes were appointed in the mission towns to maintain order. Their duty was that of police officers; they were dressed better than the others, and wore shoes and stockings, which newly appointed officers dispensed with as often as possible, choosing to go barefoot. . . . When a vacancy in the office occurred the Indians themselves were asked which one they preferred of several suggested by the priest.

Other Indians were appointed to wait on the Franciscan fathers. Some served as personal barbers to the Franciscans. Single Indian women lived inside the mission.

Here they worked under the watchful eyes of the priests. Vallejo recalled the courting practices among the Indians:

> *The women, thus separated from the men, could only be courted from without through the upper windows [of the mission] facing on the narrow village street. These windows were . . . crossed by iron bars. . . . After an Indian, in his hours of freedom from toil, had declared his affection by a sufficiently long attendance upon a certain window, it was the duty of the woman to tell the father missionary and to declare her decision. If this was favorable, the young man was asked if he was willing to contract marriage with the young woman who had confessed her preference.*

From an early age, children were taught the Catholic religion. Some children sang in the church choir. Others were taught how to play various instruments, such as the violin. These instructions were highly prized by Indian families.

The Indians were expected to follow the rules set up by the missionaries. If they violated these rules, the priests thought nothing of beating the Indians without mercy. Indeed, according to Serra himself, the idea "that spiritual fathers should punish their sons, the Indians, with blows appears to be as old as the conquest of [the Americas]." In fact, some historians have claimed that the

Fast Fact

The Spanish government had a special fund called the Pious Fund that was used to establish missions. When a mission was founded, it received about $1,000 from the Pious Fund. This money was used to buy items such as church bells, robes for the priests, seeds to plant the first crops, and gifts for the American Indians.

The Mission Style of Architecture

The missions brought a style of architecture to California that is still used today. They employed white-washed stone walls with colorful decorations. The different parts of the mission were connected by covered arcades, or corridors with archways. These were especially useful on hot summer days or during rainstorms. Residents sat in the arcades, where they could be cooled by summer breezes and escape the rain. In addition, many missions were built with a high wall pierced with small arches that had bells hung inside of them. This wall was called a *campanario*.

mission system "was a thinly disguised form of slavery."

Many of the Indians were exposed to new diseases brought by the Spanish from New Spain. These included measles and smallpox. The Indians had no immunity to these diseases and died from them. In fact, as many as 100,000 Indians may have been killed by disease or hard work at the missions.

Other Mission Work

In 1769, Governor Portolá led an expedition northward as far as San Francisco Bay. The Spanish reached San Francisco Bay on November 1. Father Juan Crespi was overawed by the bay's great size, noting that "not only all the navy of our most Catholic Majesty [the Spanish king] but those of all Europe could take shelter [here]." Since winter was rapidly arriving, the Spanish did not remain in San Francisco but headed southward to San Diego.

In 1770, a mission was established by Father Serra at Monterey, north of San Diego. Governor Portolá also established a presidio at Monterey—a small fort with a few cannons and a handful of leather jackets. Afterward, Portolá went back to New Spain. He was replaced at Monterey by Don Pedro Fages, the new governor. Two missions, however, were hardly enough to defend California from possible assault by the Russians. These missions were located 650 miles (1,046 km) from each other. Serra recognized that somehow they had to be linked together by other missions.

Nevertheless, funds and soldiers were limited. At first, Fages did not think that more missions or presidios were necessary. He characterized Serra's ideas as "nothing less than the temptation of the evil one [the Devil]." Therefore, Serra went to Mexico City. There, he convinced Gálvez of the necessity of building more missions. Before his death in 1784, Father Serra had established a total of nine missions.

In 1771, Serra moved the mission at Monterey to nearby Carmel. The soil was better there and more Indians lived in the area. Indeed, Serra liked it so much that Carmel became his headquarters. He also founded a mission south of Carmel, called San Antonio de Padua, and selected a site for another mission near Los Angeles. Two more missions were established at San Luis Obispo and San Juan Capistrano.

In 1775, a small expedition headed back to San Francisco Bay under the command of Captain Juan Bautista de Anza. Born in New Spain in 1736, he had fought against American Indians in the defense of Sonora, located in present-day northern Mexico. In 1774, de Anza had charted an overland route from Arizona (part of the Spanish Empire) to Monterey. This route avoided the winds and bad weather of the Pacific Ocean voyage from Baja to Alta California.

The following year, de Anza led a group of 245 settlers to San Francisco. In September 1776, a mission and presidio were established there. Serra dedicated the mission San Francisco de Asis in honor of St. Francis of Assisi.

Following Father Serra's death in 1784, his work was continued by Father Fermin Lasuén, who also established nine missions. All the missions were linked together by a 500-mile (805-km) roadway known as El Camino Real—"the King's Highway."

The Population of California

By 1782, there were four presidio districts with 200 soldiers divided between them. These districts were San Diego, Monterey, Santa Barbara, and San Francisco. The settlements in California were small. By 1781, the entire population was only about 600 people. Santa Barbara had a population of only about 300 people in 1790, and fewer than 150 people lived in San Francisco. Many of the residents were mestizos—people with both Spanish and American Indian parents.

In the small California settlements, the missionaries resented that the presidios had to ask the priests for food while waiting for supplies from New Spain. The soldiers, in turn, resented being asked by the missions to capture Indians who ran away to escape the harsh discipline of the Catholic priests.

Life among the soldiers was often dangerous. Sergeant Pedro Amador said that "the only compensation he had received for eighteen years' service in California was four-teen Indian arrows in his body." To the missionaries, the soldiers were rough and sometimes violent men. Many of the soldiers had been in jail in New Spain before being sent to California.

This map shows Spanish territories in the early 1800s in what would one day be the south-western United States and Mexico.

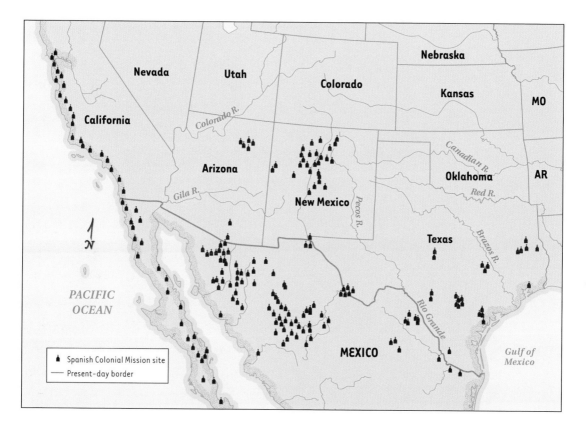

For the few soldiers who were literate, there were opportunities in California. Some rose to command important presidios. Hermengildo Sal, for example, learned how to read and write in the army. Eventually, he was placed in charge of a supply warehouse in San

Francisco. In the early 1780s, he became commandant of Santa Barbara, and later, of San Francisco.

After leaving the military, many soldiers were given large land grants in California. For example, Juan José Dominguez, who accompanied the expedition led by Governor Portolá and Father Serra, received a rancho (ranch) of 74,000 acres (29,970 ha).

Nevertheless, California remained largely under-developed. Many of the residents, known as Californios, lived on large ranchos. These Californios raised cattle and sheep. A few artisans had also come to the colony from New Spain. These included weavers, shoemakers, and potters.

Life was hard for soldiers in the California presidios of the late 1700s, such as the presidio at Monterey, shown here.

In 1791, a British explorer, George Vancouver, sailed to San Francisco from the Columbia River in present-day Washington. Later, he visited Monterey. Before leaving, Vancouver noted that the Spanish presidios in California were poorly built and difficult to defend.

An increasing number of British and Russian ships sailed on the west coast of North America to take advantage of the lucrative fur trade. Fur trappers killed sea otters that lived in the cold waters of the Pacific Ocean. Their fur pelts were taken to China, where they were traded.

U.S. trading ships also arrived in California. In 1796, the U.S. ship *Otter* arrived in Monterey. Four years later, U.S. merchant ships sailed into San Diego. One, the *Enterprise,* purchased a large supply of otter furs and then set sail for China. These traders also brought goods to sell in California, such as jewelry, furniture, and coffee. The Californios did not produce these items themselves, and very little trade was carried on between Mexico City and California. Few people from New Spain wanted to travel north to an area that they considered a rough frontier wilderness. California remained sparsely populated, much like the other colonies in the Southwest that formed part of New Spain.

Arizona

2

While the Spanish were settling California, small pueblos were also springing up in present-day Arizona. The Spanish began exploring the region during the 16th century.

In 1540, Francisco Vásquez de Coronado left Compostela, a town in New Spain on the Pacific coast. His expedition traveled northward into Arizona. Accompanying Coronado were 225 caballeros, or horsemen. Some wore coats of chain mail for protection and carried long lances. Along with 60 infantry soldiers, they were searching for the Seven Cities of Cíbola, located in present-day Arizona and New Mexico. These were rumored to contain large treasures of gold and silver.

When Coronado and his soldiers finally found Cíbola, they were disappointed. There was no treasure. The cities were merely pueblos built by Zuni Indians out of mud and adobe bricks. Some pueblos were freestanding, while others were built into the cliffs. Many were multistory structures, like ancient apartment buildings, that housed large groups of Indian families.

Coronado was considered a failure by his associates. Yet as historian Jay Wagoner wrote, "From Coronado's reports

OPPOSITE Francisco Vásquez de Coronado's search for the famed Seven Cities of Cíbola revealed that the cities were actually American Indian pueblos.

the Spanish gained a geographical knowledge of much of the great Southwest, including the Gila Valley and the Colorado Plateau regions in Arizona."

Other expeditions followed toward the end of the 1500s and the beginning of the next century. Jesuit priests also traveled among the Hopi Indians in Arizona, but the priests angered many of the local shamans, or Indian medicine men. The shamans felt that their positions were threatened by the Jesuits, especially when one of the priests cured an Indian boy of his illness. In 1680, the Hopi began a revolt in Arizona and New Mexico, led by one of their shamans known as El Popé. The Spanish were driven out of the region and did not return to Arizona until the 1690s. During the early 18th century, they established new settlements.

Father Eusebio Kino

The effort to settle Arizona during the 1700s was led by a Jesuit priest, Father Eusebio Francisco Kino. Father Kino was born in Italy in 1645 and educated by the Jesuits in nearby Austria. In 1681, the Jesuits sent him to New Spain to work in their missions. The voyage presented Father Kino with an opportunity to pursue his interest in

The Father of Arizona

Father Kino's work led to many conversions among the Pima and opened up southern Arizona to Spanish settlement. In fact, Kino is known as "the father of Arizona." He has also been called "the padre on horseback" because of all his travels to Indian pueblos in Arizona. Kino became famous among the American Indians of the Southwest. He wrote, "On journeys to very distant regions, I was met by Indians I had never seen; they would come up to me and say that they already knew me. That would happen to me even as I kept traveling farther from home." Kino added that "it is so imperative not to offend or displease any one of them."

geography. Soon after his arrival, he traveled with an expedition to Baja California and made a map of the area.

In 1687, Kino went from Mexico City to Sonora to work among the Pima Indians. In Sonora, he set up many missions devoted to converting the Pima to Christianity. He also realized that the Indians' spiritual growth depended on caring for their practical needs. From his primary mission in Sonora, he brought herds of cattle to the other missions to feed the local Indians. According to historian Jay Wagoner, he also "attempted to assure his converts a regular food supply by instructing them in the best methods of crop raising and animal husbandry."

In 1700, Father Kino established his first mission in Arizona, along the Santa Cruz River. Located at Bac in southern Arizona, it was called San Xavier del Bac. Another mission was established soon afterward at Los Santos Angeles de Guevavi, south of San Xavier del Bac. Father Kino wanted to establish more missions in Arizona. He recognized that the Pima were important allies for the Spanish. They helped to defend the area against the Apache, who were constantly raiding Spanish cattle herds. However, the Spanish government was too preoccupied with wars in Europe to spend much money on defending a frontier area such as Arizona.

Successors to Father Kino

Father Kino died in 1711. "So effective had the padre become," wrote Jay Wagoner, "in associating the Pima with the Spanish . . . that he was said to be equal to a garrison of soldiers on the frontier." The missionaries who came after Kino seemed unable to develop the same close relationships that he had maintained with the Indians. During the 1730s, Father Johann Grazhoffer began working among the Pima at the Guevavi mission. The Pima did not like Grazhoffer—they poisoned his food and killed him in 1733.

Father Phelipe Segesser served the Pima who lived at the mission in San Xavier del Bac during the 1730s. He was a keen observer of their customs. He observed that the Pima were an agricultural people who grew maize (corn) as the main food in their diet. Their diet also included ox meat, mouse, and snake meat. Apache warriors regularly raided Pima pueblos but were beaten back by the Pima, who frequently conducted their own attacks on the Apache villages. Then the women would stage victory dances, carrying the scalps of the fallen Apache braves.

During these and other dances, Father Segesser wrote,

the Pima paint themselves with yellow, red, or white paint so that they more resemble specters than human beings. . . . Dances occur . . . every night, accompanied by singing or yowling with no articulated words. . . . The nightly dances make most Pimas lazy and inactive and they lounge about unless the father [priest] drives them to work like donkeys. . . .

From the tone of his writing, it is clear that Segesser had little patience with the customs of the Pima. In turn, the Indians often showed little respect for the padres. A brief revolt among the Pima broke out in 1734, which only stopped when Spanish troops arrived to overpower the Indian warriors.

During the 1740s, Father Jacobo Sedelmayr traveled through southern Arizona. He visited the Pima and the Papago Indians, converting many of them to Christianity. Like Father Kino, Sedelmayr was interested in exploring the area. He recognized the importance of Arizona to the Spanish. He urged that they put military outposts on the Gila and the Colorado Rivers in Arizona to safeguard a land route from New Spain to California. He also emphasized that more missions were necessary among the Pima to strengthen their alliance with Spain and protect the area from the Apaches.

This colored woodcut from the 1800s shows a Pima village in the desert of the present-day U.S. Southwest.

Unfortunately, Spain neglected this alliance, and the Pima revolted in 1751. One reason for the revolt was the discovery of silver in Arizona. Thousands of miners poured into Arizona to participate in the silver strike. These immigrants seemed threatening to the Pima, who feared that they might be attacked. In addition, the Pima resented the harsh treatment they sometimes received from the Spanish priests. During the revolt, the Pima killed about 100 Spanish settlers as well as several priests. A Spanish army rushed north and finally put down the revolt.

Father Middendorff and Father Garcés

In order to protect the settlers in Arizona, the Spanish established a presidio at Tubac in 1752. Soldiers were sent to Tubac to man the presidio, and settlers established a town outside its gates. About 400 Spanish settlers were living there by 1757. Catholic missionaries also continued their work among the American Indians in Arizona. In 1756, Father Bernardo Middendorff established a new mission at San Agustin del Tucson. Middendorff accompanied the Spanish soldiers who were conducting raids against the Papago and other Indians.

The missions at Tucson and other locations in Arizona were constantly threatened with attack during the next decade. In 1768, the Apache destroyed part of the mission at San Xavier del Bac. Later that year, this mission was taken over by Father Francisco Garcés, a member of the Franciscan order. Garcés was not only a missionary but an explorer, like Father Kino. During the 1770s, Garcés traveled along the Gila River, through southern Arizona, and into California. In 1774, he helped guide the expedition led by Juan Bautista de Anza—who was the commander at Tubac—that found a land route to California. Garcés also accompanied de Anza part of the way on his expedition to California in 1775.

While de Anza headed northward, Garcés stayed behind on the Colorado River, between Arizona and California. Near the site of the modern city of Yuma, Arizona, he began to set up a small mission. He was assisted by the Yuma Indians who lived in the area. The Spanish regarded an outpost on the Colorado River as essential to protect the land route from New Spain to California.

While work on the mission was underway, Garcés traveled among the Yuma, trying to convert them to Christianity. By 1780, the Spanish had begun to establish two settlements around Yuma, each consisting of a mission and a presidio. According to Wagoner, "Garcés and Father Juan Barraneche . . . the young missionary sent to assist him, directed the construction of a church out of logs and mud. Nearby, the soldiers built a guardhouse and one-room cabins where they would live when their wives and children arrived."

The soldiers were not as kind to the Yuma as Father Garcés was. The Spanish at the presidio set up farms outside the walls, often taking lands that the Indians used to plant their own crops. In addition, the soldiers allowed their livestock to run loose and trample the Indians' corn. These practices led to tension between the Yuma and the Spanish garrison.

Tucson

Meanwhile, the Spanish had been building the settlement at Tucson. During the early 1770s, Garcés, who had replaced Father Middendorff, directed the construction of the first mission. This mission, which was built for defense, had "sophisticated rounded lookout towers at the corners," according to historian Kieran McCarty. The mission was completed just in time to fend off an attack by the Apache in February 1771. By the next year, a church was under construction. Finally, in 1775, Colonel Hugo O'Conor laid out a presidio.

Construction of the new presidio continued under the direction of Captain Don Pedro de Allande y Saabedra. At first, logs were used to build a temporary fort. These were eventually replaced by adobe. The presidio was completed in 1783. It contained a church, stables for the horses, and cabins for the soldiers. They drilled in a large square known as the Plaza de las Armas. Cannons mounted on the surrounding walls of the presidio protected the garrison against possible Indian attacks.

An assault at Tucson by 350 Apache warriors was driven back by Captain Allande in 1779. Violence also erupted in western Arizona. The Yuma tribe revolted in 1781, killing Father Garcés, who was then working at Yuma, as well as other settlers living there. As a result, the Spanish decided to abandon the area along the Colorado River. Instead, they focused their attention on Tucson. Here, attacks by the Apache continued during the 1780s, and the Spanish retaliated by attacking Apache villages.

By 1786, the continuing Apache raids made the Spanish realize that their military campaign was not working. Therefore, they tried a new strategy to deal with the Apache: While continuing the military campaigns, the Spanish also signed peace treaties with some of the Apache to persuade them to live in villages near Tucson. By the 1790s, some Apache were living outside of Tucson. A few settlers had also begun to arrive at the new town. The total population, including soldiers and Indians, reached about 1,000 by 1795.

Despite being vulnerable to attacks by the Apache in the 1700s, the mission at San Xavier del Bac was left alone by the American Indians.

In order to maintain peace with the Apache, the garrison provided them with annual presents. According to historian John Kessell,

Of 300 beef cattle slaughtered annually at Tucson, 130 were consigned at government expense, along with sugar and tobacco, to Apaches who came and went at the peace camp downriver from the presidio. Although Apache warfare had decreased notably . . . soldiers and settlers still sallied forth on joint campaigns.

The settlement at Tucson would continue to grow during the early 19th century. Meanwhile, the Spanish were establishing settlements to the east, in present-day New Mexico. 🔳

New Mexico

3

The settlement of New Mexico by the Spanish was motivated by several forces: the search for gold, the desire to convert the local American Indians, and the defense of New Spain.

In 1540, Coronado led the first Spanish expedition to New Mexico, looking for gold in the Seven Cities of Cíbola. Finding no treasure, he returned to New Spain. In 1581, a Franciscan priest, Father Agustin Rodríguez, led another expedition consisting of a few soldiers and several Franciscans to New Mexico. Rodríguez hoped to convert the Indians to Christianity. He traveled along the Pecos River, reaching Taos in northern New Mexico. The Franciscans met with Pueblo Indians, who seemed interested in listening to the message of Christianity. However, the Pueblo also feared that the priests were the leading edge of a military invasion, like Coronado's, so they turned on the Franciscans, including Rodríguez, and killed them.

In 1598, the Spanish launched another attempt to establish an outpost in New Mexico—and to find gold or silver. This expedition was led by Juan de Oñate, a successful silver mine owner. Indeed, Oñate was wealthy enough to finance

OPPOSITE Pueblo Indians of New Mexico in the 1800s are shown participating in a burial ceremony in this woodcut.

the expedition himself. He led a group of about 600 settlers from Mexico City to the Rio Grande, where they established a small town called San Gabriel. This was the first capital of New Mexico.

Later that year, Oñate took a group of soldiers on a mission to explore the area around San Gabriel. Meanwhile, the town was threatened by the Acoma Indian tribe. The Acoma killed Oñate's nephew, Juan de Zaldivar, who was bringing troops to join his uncle's expedition. Oñate eventually defeated the Acoma—but by this time, the settlers had become frustrated with their new lives at San Gabriel. No gold and silver could be found, and the settlers were constantly threatened by local Indians. Before Oñate returned to San Gabriel, most of them had gone home to Mexico City.

Oñate is known as "the father of New Mexico" because he established the first settlement there. However, he was soon replaced by a new governor, Don Pedro de Peralta. In 1610, Peralta moved what was left of the settlement at San Gabriel to a new location. Peralta called it Santa Fe, one of the oldest permanent settlements in North America.

> **Fast Fact**
>
> Historians are not certain how the town of Santa Fe obtained its name. Peralta may have named it after a city in Spain or adopted the Spanish words that mean "holy faith," *santa fe.*

The Missionaries

During the rest of the 1600s, approximately 250 Franciscan missionaries came to New Mexico to convert the Indians. In New Mexico, this century is known as the Great Missionary

Era. The Spanish monarchy paid millions of dollars for the missionaries to bring Christianity to the Pueblo. As historian Marc Simmons wrote, "The expenditure of so vast a sum on what was purely a humanitarian undertaking underscored the king's commitment to the spread of the True Faith."

In their effort to bring Christianity to the Pueblo, the Franciscans tried to stamp out the Indians' traditional religious beliefs. They also threatened the positions of the Pueblo medicine men, the religious leaders of the villages. The Pueblo, on the other hand, saw no reason why the two sets of beliefs could not be blended together. This disagreement led to conflicts between the Indians and the priests.

In 1675, Governor Juan Francisco Treviño rounded up over 40 medicine men who opposed the work of the Spanish priests. Three of the medicine men were hanged, while the others were severely whipped and sent to jail. In retaliation, the medicine men planned a revolt against the Spanish.

Kachinas

The traditional Pueblo religion centered on kachinas, the divine spirits of dead Pueblo Indians. The kachinas appeared when the Pueblo performed sacred rituals. These ceremonies were performed in underground kivas, or caves, that were decorated with murals depicting the kachinas. The Pueblo wore kachina masks portraying the sacred spirits. The spirits were also represented by kachina dolls carved by the Pueblo for their children. The kachinas blessed the Pueblo people, bringing them plentiful rain and rich harvests. In New Mexico, the Franciscans tried to end the kachina ceremonies and destroy the kivas, but they were unsuccessful.

Most of the Pueblo living in New Mexico supported the revolt. Throughout the century, the Spanish priests had forced the Pueblo to work at the missions that had been established at the Indian villages. Indians who disobeyed were often whipped and beaten. Spanish governors had also established the *encomienda* system in New Mexico. Under this system, the Pueblo granted their labor to the Spaniards and paid them tribute in corn and clothing. In return, the Spanish government was responsible for protecting and converting the Indians. This same system had existed since the 16th century in the region that is now Mexico. Although the encomienda system was not officially a type of slavery, the Indians frequently suffered under brutal living and working conditions.

An American Indian on a Caribbean sugar plantation suffers cruelly at the hands of the Spanish under the encomienda system.

In addition, Spanish settlers in New Mexico were permitted to use *repartimiento*—a system that required the Pueblo to work Spanish lands. The Indians were supposed to be paid and fed, but, according to historian Marc Simmons, "many Spaniards avoided paying wages; they held out on rations . . . they often took the Pueblos at harvest time, when the Indians were desperately needed for work at home; and, most oppressive of all, they offended native women."

In 1680, the Pueblo staged their massive revolt. This was part of the same revolt that broke out among the Hopi in Arizona that year. The Pueblo overran the Spanish settlements, home to about 2,500 people. More than 400 settlers were killed. Many of the remaining settlers fled to Santa Fe, where they took refuge in the heavily defended home of the governor, Antonio de Otermín. The Spanish held out for nine days. "I had lost much blood from two arrow wounds which I had received in the face," de Otermín wrote later, "and a remarkable gunshot wound in the chest on the day before." The governor gathered up his supplies of water and horses and brought the settlers together in a caravan. Protected by the Spanish troops, they fought their way out of Santa Fe and headed south. Eventually, they arrived in El Paso, a Spanish settlement on the border of New Spain. Thus Spain lost New Mexico and also abandoned Arizona at this time.

The Recovery of New Mexico

The Spanish abandoned New Mexico for more than a decade, but they had not given up on their efforts to control the area. Spain still believed that its mission was to convert

American Indians to Christianity. Spanish governors, like de Otermín, also believed that New Mexico was essential to the defense of the Spanish Empire. Bands of Apache in Arizona and New Mexico could easily launch attacks southward, threatening Spanish settlements in New Spain.

By the 1690s, the leaders of the Pueblo revolt were dead. The Indian villages had lost the unity that had enabled them to gather a large army to defeat the Spanish. In 1691, Governor Don Diego de Vargas led a Spanish expedition into New Mexico to recover the area. De Vargas drove the Pueblo out of Santa Fe and took back control of many of the Indian towns. He also agreed to respect the Indian religion, which won him the support of many Pueblo. By this time, the Pueblo population had declined by more than one-half, to about 14,000 tribal members, owing to disease and attacks by the Apache.

By the early 18th century, the Spanish had established new settlements in New Mexico. Albuquerque, located south of Santa Fe, was founded in 1706. (Today, Albuquerque is the largest city in New Mexico.) Strong presidios were also built in Santa Fe and El Paso. These were manned by troops sent from Mexico City.

Nevertheless, life on the frontier was very dangerous because of attacks by bands of Apache, Comanche, Navajo, and Ute. Spanish settlers who came to New Mexico set up ranches where they raised sheep, cattle, and horses. Many of these settlements were located near major towns, like Santa Fe or Albuquerque. Others were established near Indian pueblos, like Taos in northern New Mexico. The settlers hoped that in case of attack, they could flee to the nearby towns and villages for protection. Many still lost their lives during raids by the Indians, who drove off cattle and horses from the settlers' ranchos.

In 1774, a band of 200 Comanche attacked Albuquerque. Spanish settlers and Pueblo Indians were killed, and the Comanche drove off the town's sheep and horses. South of Albuquerque, the Navajo drove off another large sheep herd. As a result of the attacks, settlers left their homes and ranchos and headed for the protection of the villages. Father Francisco Atanasio Domínguez, who visited Taos, said it was so heavily defended that it looked like "those walled cities with bastions and towers that are described in the Bible."

In 1776, the same year that the North American colonies declared their independence from Britain, the Spanish government decided to increase its defenses along the New

Teodoro de Croix

Teodoro de Croix (1730–1792) spent his entire adult life in the Spanish military. In 1766, after his first 20 years of service, his uncle, the Marqués de Croix, became the viceroy of New Spain. Teodoro was named governor of Acapulco, on the west coast. In 1777, he became the new commandant general of the Interior Provinces. In this position, Croix strengthened the forts and towns along the Spanish frontier. Arriving in Texas in 1778, he increased the number of Spanish militia (citizen-soldiers) defending the colony against American Indians. In 1783, Croix left New Spain to become viceroy of the Spanish colony of Peru.

Mexico frontier. New Mexico and Arizona became part of the Interior Provinces, which included 2,000 miles (3,218 km) of territory from California to Louisiana. These provinces were placed in charge of General Teodoro de Croix. He brought 2,000 additional troops northward. These troops were essential, Croix realized. He wrote to an official in Mexico City, "It is evident that with small, poorly arranged forces scattered over great distances . . . advantageous operations of war could not be undertaken nor can an extensive country of unhappy and sparse settlements be defended." In 1778, New Mexico also received a new governor, Juan Bautista de Anza, who had led the expeditions to California a few years earlier.

Battle and Treaty

None of the Spanish leaders along the frontier had more experience than de Anza. He realized that the Apache and Comanche were an enormous threat to the future of New Mexico. The two tribes had about 5,000 warriors to send against the Spanish, and de Anza wrote that

> *to these should be added an equal number of women, who, if they do not make war in the same way as the men, aid it in whatever actions the Apaches under-take. . . . Thus they form regularly a reserve corps, round up the horses while the men attack our troops, and . . . the enemy succeeds, by increasing the number of individuals, in creating the well-founded idea that they are more formidable.*

The new governor and General de Croix decided to focus their efforts on the Comanche. Governor de Anza planned to lead a campaign against them, which he hoped would stop their raids and bring them into alliance with the Spanish. Then they could work together to defeat the Apache.

During the summer of 1779, de Anza launched his expedition from Santa Fe. His attack was aimed at the Comanche leader, Chief Cuerno Verde ("Green Horn"). De Anza said that Cuerno Verde was "the scourge of this kingdom, who has exterminated many towns, killing hundreds and making as many prisoners whom he afterwards sacrificed in cold blood." De Anza led the largest Spanish army that had ever been launched on an expedition against American Indians—more than 600 men, both Spanish troops and Pueblo allies.

Juan Bautista de Anza, who became governor of New Mexico in 1778, signed peace treaties with the Comanche, Navajo, and Ute, helping to bring peace to the frontier.

Hoping to surprise the Comanche, de Anza led his troops along the western side of the Rocky Mountains, where they were out of sight of the Comanche on the other side. Then he crossed through a pass and struck the Comanche villages. Cuerno Verde was not there, but de Anza learned that he would soon be returning. The Spanish laid a trap for the Comanche chief, who rode into the ambush. "They were without other recourse," de Anza wrote; "they sprang to the ground and, entrenched behind their horses, made in this manner a defense as brave as it was glorious." However, the Comanche warriors, including Chief Cuerno Verde, were wiped out.

This was a major victory for the Spanish. Yet the Indian wars did not stop immediately. The Apache raids continued, and Governor de Anza gave orders for another program to

Frontier Families

The harsh conditions on the Western frontier had a major impact on colonial families. In the more settled areas of New Spain, such as the capital, Mexico City, men and women fulfilled traditional roles, like the people of Europe. A man was considered the head of his family. A woman ran the household, cooked the food, and raised the family's children.

On the frontier, however, family roles were different. One reason was that there were fewer people available. Therefore, many women had to work in the fields, just like their husbands. Many men were killed defending their homes from Indian raids, leaving an unusually large number of widows on the frontier. Widows were then forced to take on new roles, running farms, ranches, or stores following the deaths of their husbands.

defend the settlers. He wanted them to relocate their farms so they could gather together at strong outposts. These outposts, according to Spanish officials, would include "ample square plazas of at least twenty families each in the form of redoubts . . . [with] ramparts for the range of the short firelocks [guns] that are in use." The Spanish settlers on the ranchos around Albuquerque and Taos agreed to follow the orders and relocate to these towns.

Finally, during the 1780s, the Comanche decided to make peace with the Spanish because they were tired of fighting. Comanche villages had been attacked by other Indians, such as the Apache. In addition, disease had reduced the number of Comanche warriors. The negotiations began at Taos in July 1785 and continued until early the following year. De Anza wanted assurances from the Comanche leaders that all the villages would agree to peace.

Finally, in February 1786, the Comanche leaders traveled to Santa Fe, where they met with Governor de Anza. De Anza insisted that as part of the treaty, the Comanche also make peace with the Ute. The Comanche agreed to the governor's terms. Later in February, de Anza went to a gathering of the Comanche to finalize the treaty. "All, one by one, came up to embrace him with such excessive expressions of affection and respect that they were by no means appropriate to his rank and station." Nevertheless, the governor was happy to embrace his former enemies.

In addition to a treaty with the Comanche, de Anza signed similar agreements with the Ute and Navajo. These treaties helped bring peace to the New Mexico frontier. A year later, the governor left office because of illness. He died in 1788. Nevertheless, the peace in New Mexico continued.

By the end of the 18th century, Santa Fe was the largest Spanish settlement in the Southwest. Approximately 5,000 settlers lived there. Wealthy Spanish settlers owned large ranches outside the city.

Merchants traded with Indians along the Mississippi River. They also established communications with Texas and the new Spanish colony of Louisiana. The new routes to these colonies were pioneered by a Frenchman who had lived among the Indians, Pedro Vial. In 1786 and 1787, he blazed a trail from San Antonio, Texas, to Santa Fe. For a short period, he settled in Santa Fe, but, growing restless again, he offered to establish another trade route between New Mexico and Louisiana. He arrived in Louisiana later in 1787. His destination was the trading center of Natchitoches, located on the Red River in western Louisiana. The Spanish had now linked their empire from the Southwest to Louisiana.

Louisiana and the Spanish Empire

4

The colony of Louisiana was founded in 1682 by the French explorer René-Robert Cavelier, Sieur de La Salle. With an expedition of 50 men, La Salle traveled from the Great Lakes—part of French Canada—down the Mississippi River to its mouth. The French regarded Louisiana as the southern outpost of a vast empire that stretched from Canada down through Illinois Country and along the Mississippi River to the Gulf of Mexico.

After La Salle's expedition, the French expanded their colony to include present-day Louisiana, Alabama, and Mississippi. They established settlements at Natchez in Mississippi, Mobile in Alabama, and New Orleans, which became the capital of Louisiana in 1722. French governors tried to maintain close relationships with the powerful American Indian tribes in Louisiana, including the Choctaw and the Chickasaw. These allies were critical to defending the colony against possible attacks by the British. Since Louisiana was a small colony, with only about 3,000 settlers, it was too weak to defend itself.

OPPOSITE René-Robert Cavelier, Sieur de La Salle (center), is shown here claiming Louisiana for King Louis XIV of France in 1682.

The Louisiana Territory, shown here, was much bigger than the modern state of Louisiana is today and included an area that reached to the border of Canada.

In the mid-18th century, a war broke out between France and Great Britain in North America, known as the French and Indian War (1754–1763). Partway through the war, Spain allied itself with the French against the British. Nevertheless, the French were defeated, losing control of Canada in the early 1760s. In 1762, before they signed a peace treaty with Britain the following year, the French gave New Orleans and western Louisiana to Spain. This was a reward for Spanish assistance during the war and an effort to keep the territory out of British control.

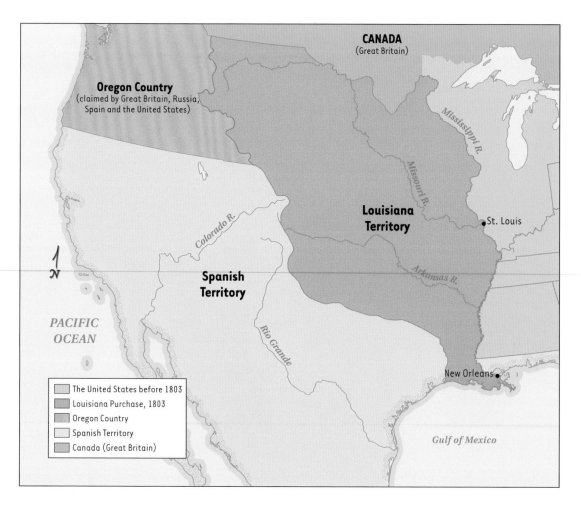

Spanish Louisiana

Spain did not occupy Louisiana until 1766. In that year, the Spanish sent Governor Don Antonio de Ulloa and 90 soldiers to bring Spanish rule to the area. It was hardly enough to govern such a vast territory. Ulloa hoped to have the services of acting French governor Captain Charles Aubrey and his 300 soldiers, but the French were unwilling to join the Spanish army. Ulloa also faced many angry French colonists who did not want to become part of the Spanish Empire. Ulloa irritated the French even further when he tried to run the colony without the Superior Council, a group of leading French colonists who had ruled Louisiana along with the French governor. In addition, Ulloa tried to put an end to smuggling by wealthy French merchants who were bringing in goods from British traders to sell in New Orleans.

In 1768, the French political leaders of New Orleans staged a revolt against Governor Ulloa. These leaders included members of the Superior Council, such as the colony's attorney general, Nicolas Chauvin de La Frenière. While Aubrey and his soldiers stood by, the French leaders drove the governor out of town and brought an end, they hoped, to Spanish rule.

Spain was not prepared to lose Louisiana so easily. The Spanish regarded the colony as a front line of defense against the British, protecting Spain's other colonies in New Spain and the Southwest. In 1769, Spain sent General Alejandro O'Reilly and 2,000 troops to Louisiana to regain control of the colony. O'Reilly reached New Orleans in July.

Alejandro O'Reilly

Alejandro O'Reilly (1725–1794) was born in Ireland but left the country as a young man because there were few jobs available there. He joined the Spanish army and later served at Havana, Cuba, one of Spain's most important military posts in the New World. In 1765, he was sent to the Spanish colony of Puerto Rico, where he established a strong colonial militia that helped protect the island from attack. Because of O'Reilly's outstanding record in the Spanish military, he was promoted to lieutenant general and chosen to lead the army that put down the French revolt in Louisiana in 1769. Once O'Reilly reached New Orleans, he established its cabildo. He tried to soothe the feelings of the French citizens by reducing the size of his army and keeping French commanders in charge of the important posts in Louisiana. General O'Reilly returned to Spain in late 1770.

He arrested the leaders of the revolt and brought them to trial. Several of them, including La Frenière, were executed by a firing squad.

The New Spanish Government

General O'Reilly wasted little time in establishing a new government in New Orleans. The Superior Council was replaced by a *cabildo*, or city government. Over the next four decades, well-to-do French and Spanish settlers purchased seats on the cabildo. O'Reilly awarded the first positions to Frenchmen who had been loyal to Spain. Some of these positions were held for life, while other *regidores*, or cabildo members, were replaced annually.

New Orleans was the center of the colony, and its regidores had important responsibilities in running the government. Chief among them was collecting taxes. The Spanish imposed taxes on imports such as wine and liquor. Raisins and chocolates, special favorites of New Orleans residents, were also imported to the colony from

Europe and taxed. Grain was taxed by the cabildo as well. The climate in New Orleans was too wet to grow wheat and produce grain. Therefore, grain was imported from Illinois Country and baked into bread by the bakers in New Orleans. As part of their responsibilities, the regidores had to ensure a steady supply of grain and beef into New Orleans to feed the residents of the city. The cabildo contracted with local butchers to supply the beef and then taxed their produce.

Beef, vegetables, fish, and other products were sold at local markets that the cabildo established in New Orleans. The cabildo charged merchants to set up shop in the markets. The cabildo also appointed inspectors to ensure that all the produce sold in the markets was fresh. The inspectors verified that New Orleans merchants were charging their customers honestly for meat and other products.

Employing inspectors was one of the many services provided by the cabildo with the tax money it collected. Another important service was maintaining the levees along the Mississippi River. These dams, constructed of dirt, rose 15 feet (4.6 m) above the river. They were designed to protect New Orleans from being flooded when the river overflowed, which it did regularly. The broad levee outside New Orleans became a popular gathering place for the residents of the city, who could walk on the levee along the river and watch the sailing ships that had tied up there while bringing goods to New Orleans from Europe. The levee was described by a contemporary observer as "a handsome raised gravel walk, planted with orange-trees; and in the summer-time served for a mall, and in an evening was always a fashionable resort for the beaux and belles of the place."

The port city of New Orleans was the center of Louisiana life throughout the history of the colony. It is still the capital of Louisiana today.

Sanitation was a continuing problem in New Orleans. Residents threw their garbage out windows into the street. Dead animals were allowed to remain in the streets and rot. One observer described the streets this way: "During the greater part of the year, they are a common sewer; a sink of nastiness, dirt, and corruption." The streets often flowed with water from the Mississippi River. The cabildo built wooden sidewalks that enabled residents to avoid the muddy streets, but when the wood rotted, the sidewalks were not repaired.

To protect the residents of New Orleans, the cabildo hired watchmen. They patrolled the city at night and lit the candles in the streetlights that had been installed to brighten the dark streets. The lights and the watchmen protected residents from being attacked by criminals who might be lurking in the darkness. In addition, Spain garrisoned New Orleans with troops to defend the city against possible attack by American Indians or the British. These troops paraded on the Plaza de Armas, located at the center of New Orleans. Around the plaza were a Spanish church, the city jail, and the building where the cabildo met.

Residents of the City

Many wealthy residents of New Orleans made their money as merchants and planters. Outside New Orleans lay large plantations that grew rice, indigo, tobacco, and sugar. These products were exported to Europe. Indigo was especially prized by European royalty because the blue dye that came from the indigo plants was used to give royal robes their rich color.

Plantation owners spent much of the year on their estates, supervising the work of their field hands. In the fall, after the harvest, the plantation owners lived in New Orleans, where they enjoyed the social season in the city. Well-to-do residents held weekly balls where men and women dressed in rich clothing and danced until the early hours of the morning.

Schools in New Orleans

During the 1700s, several schools for children were established in New Orleans. By the end of the century, there were eight private schools with a total student population of 400. One school was strictly for girls. It was run by an order of Ursuline nuns who lived in a convent in New Orleans. Young men could also attend a military school, where they trained to become officers in the Spanish garrison stationed in New Orleans. In 1772, the Spanish opened a free public school for children whose parents could not afford to send them to private school. About 150 students attended the school, where classes were taught in Spanish and French.

The wealthy enjoyed spending their free time gambling or drinking: There were more than 90 taverns in New Orleans. A theater opened in 1792. This theater was operated by two brothers, Jean-Marie and Louis-Alexander Henry. Some of the theatergoers, unfortunately, became unruly during performances. As a result, the Henry brothers posted a sign in the theater. It read,

No one will be allowed to throw or pretend to throw oranges or anything else, be it in the theater or in any other part of the hall, nor, in a word, shall anyone be allowed to start quarrels with his neighbor or with anyone; nor shall anyone insult anybody or come to blows or speak ill of another in order to stir up trouble.

The majority of residents in New Orleans could not afford to live in fine houses or attend the theater. Many of them were storeowners, small merchants, or artisans, such as carpenters and blacksmiths. Some worked along the wharves unloading ships that came into New Orleans. Others operated as boatmen along the Mississippi River, bringing grain and other products from Illinois Country. These settlers made a modest living. Their homes in New Orleans were wooden shacks located along muddy streets far back from the river. Other settlers lived outside the city, where they carved out small farms along the Mississippi River.

Fast Fact

One of the most famous parts of New Orleans is the French Quarter. When New Orleans was destroyed by fires in the late 18th century, the Spanish cabildo paid to rebuild it. The new French Quarter used a style of architecture that shows a strong Spanish influence.

Among the cabildo's sources of revenue was the chimney tax. The regidores taxed homeowners for every chimney in their houses. Wealthy residents had large houses with several chimneys, so they paid high chimney taxes. The homes of the well-to-do were usually made of brick with large porches, or verandas, stretching around them. The first floors were raised several feet above the ground to prevent the houses from being flooded. Many of these houses were located on narrow strips of ground along the Mississippi River.

African Americans in Louisiana

The French began bringing African slaves into Louisiana during the first quarter of the 18th century. The Africans lived in villages near the west coast of Africa. Here, they cultivated rice and indigo; they would eventually help introduce the cultivation of these crops into Louisiana. Men, women, and children were captured by African slave traders, brought to the African coast, and sold there to European slavers. These slave captains

Fires and Hurricanes

During the period of Spanish rule, New Orleans was repeatedly struck by fires. In 1788, a serious fire broke out when candles in a resident's house lit the curtains. Almost 80 percent of the city was destroyed—over 800 homes.

The rebuilding began immediately, but it was cut short in 1794, when another fire broke out and destroyed more than 200 buildings. The cabildo urged homeowners to rebuild with brick instead of cypress wood, but few settlers could afford the extra expense of brick homes.

Hurricanes were also frequent occurrences in New Orleans. Severe hurricanes struck the city in 1779, 1780, and 1793. Ten people were killed in the hurricane of 1780, and 22 died in the hurricane of 1793.

transported the Africans across the Atlantic Ocean to colonies in the Americas.

During the trip across the Atlantic, known as the Middle Passage, the slaves were kept below decks most of the time. Hundreds of slaves were chained in the ship's hold in foul conditions. Some of the slaves became sick and died. Others, when they were brought up on deck to be fed, refused to eat. A few captives jumped overboard and drowned rather than spend the rest of their lives as slaves.

The Africans who reached Louisiana were sold as slaves to plantation owners around New Orleans and at other settlements. By the time of the Spanish takeover in 1762, there were about 5,000 slaves in Louisiana. The black population rose to over 24,000 by 1800, largely because the Spanish continued to import slaves to work on the plantations.

The lives of the slaves were strictly controlled by a series of laws known as the Code Noir (Black Code), established by the French and followed by the Spanish. The Code Noir prevented slaves on different plantations from meeting together in a group. Slaves were also forbidden to carry weapons or travel from one plantation to another without a pass signed by their masters. These laws were designed to prevent the slaves, who far outnumbered the white settlers, from starting a rebellion.

French slave owners controlled the lives of their slaves using a set of laws known as the Code Noir (Black Code).

Small uprisings did occur in 1791 and 1792. Another major uprising in 1795 was uncovered by the Spanish authorities before it began. The Spanish militia killed 25 slaves while they were being rounded up, and many others were hanged.

During the 1790s, a slave revolt broke out in the French colony of Haiti on the island of Santo Domingo in the Caribbean. The government was overthrown, many white settlers were killed, and others fled the island. The Spanish feared that a similar revolt might occur in Louisiana. One settler later wrote,

> *I can recall when our position in this colony was ever so critical, when we used to go to bed only if armed to the teeth. Often then, I would go to sleep with the most sinister thoughts creeping into mind, taking heed of the dreadful calamities of Saint Domingue [Santo Domingo], and of the germs of insurrection only too widespread among our own slaves.*

A major reason why a revolt seemed possible in Louisiana was the harshness with which many slaves were treated by their masters. The Code Noir was supposed to protect slaves, specifying that they were to be well-fed and properly housed. Yet many slaves were given meager amounts of food to eat and were whipped if they disobeyed their masters. The Code Noir permitted masters to sell children older than seven to other plantations. As a result, parents and children might never see each other again.

To prevent this harsh fate, some slaves escaped from the plantations into the swamps. These *cimarrons,* or maroons, as they were called, established African-American communities in the vast swamplands that their former masters feared to enter. There, the maroons built huts and supported themselves by hunting and fishing.

Under the Code Noir, slaves were allowed one day off each week. They could also maintain their own small plots of land where they grew vegetables. Slaves journeyed into New Orleans and sold their produce at the Congo Market. A substantial number of slaves eventually saved the several hundred dollars necessary to buy their own freedom. Others were granted their freedom in wills signed by their masters. In 1763, there were about 3,600 free African Americans in New Orleans. This population grew to almost 20,000 by 1800.

The Impact of Spanish Rule

Under the Spanish, New Orleans flourished. Spain invested large amounts of money in the colony. The Spanish paid immigrants to leave Europe and relocate in Louisiana. About 2,000 settlers came from the Canary Islands, off the coast of western Europe. Others came from Canada. The Spanish government also established important trade privileges for the merchants of New Orleans that helped turn the city into a major trading port. According to historian Gwendolyn Midlo Hall, "Louisiana tobacco enjoyed a monopoly of the Mexican market. Louisiana was given a monopoly of the production of wooden boxes in which sugar was exported throughout the Spanish Empire. Only Louisiana sugar boxes could be used in the Spanish Empire ports touching the Gulf of Mexico." These boxes were made from the wood of cypress trees, which grew abundantly in Louisiana.

During the American Revolution (1775–1783) between Britain and its colonies along the Atlantic coast of North America, France and Spain supported the colonial armies. Louisiana governor Bernardo de Gálvez led a Spanish army westward to capture posts that had been taken by Britain as a result of the French and Indian War. These included Natchez and Mobile. When the American Revolution ended, Spain retained these settlements and expanded the Louisiana colony.

During the 1780s, the economy of Louisiana grew, but prosperity began to disappear after 1789. In France, the French Revolution (1789–1799) broke out, overthrowing the king, Louis XVI. King Louis and his wife, Marie Antoinette, were eventually executed along with many other members of the French nobility. The revolution disrupted the market for Louisiana's products, such as indigo and sugar. In Europe, many monarchs joined together to fight against the new French government. Eventually, a new military hero emerged who defeated the armies allied against France. Napoleon Bonaparte took control of France and began to expand its borders as a result of his stunning military victories against the nations of Europe.

Napoleon also dreamed of reestablishing French influence in the New World. In 1800, he signed a treaty with Spain that called for the French to take back control of Louisiana. In return, the Spanish received some land in Europe. Napoleon also hoped to retake Haiti. Since Spain was an ally of France, Napoleon continued to let the

Spanish appoint governors and run New Orleans through the Spanish cabildo.

Napoleon's plans in the Caribbean were unsuccessful. By 1803, he had given up any hope of reestablishing the French in the New World. Meanwhile, the U.S. government had become interested in acquiring Louisiana. Farmers in territories such as Kentucky, Missouri, and Tennessee were sending their produce down the Mississippi River to New Orleans for shipment abroad. Some U.S. citizens had even moved into northern Louisiana. U.S. merchants also carried on a brisk trade with the residents of New Orleans. Recognizing that U.S. migration westward could not be stopped, Spain hoped to absorb some of the frontier families into the Spanish Empire.

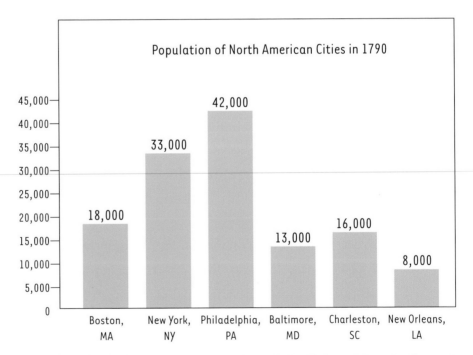

Despite its importance to the Spanish, English, and French, the port city of New Orleans still had a population of only 8,000 in 1790.

In 1803, President Thomas Jefferson acquired Louisiana from Napoleon. The Louisiana Purchase included almost 800,000 acres (324,000 ha) of new territory. With the sale of Louisiana, the Spanish lost the buffer that they had wanted to protect their territory in present-day Mexico and the Southwest. This created new tensions with the United States and significant problems for the Spanish, especially in Texas. 🔲

Texas

5

T he Spanish settled Texas in much the same way that they occupied the rest of the Southwest. Missionaries and soldiers claimed the area for Spain to provide a defensive buffer against the French along the Mississippi River in Louisiana. The Spanish began establishing missions in present-day Texas during the last part of the 17th century. Don Alonso de León, governor of Coahuila in northern New Spain, led an expedition of about 100 soldiers into Texas in 1689. He marched into Texas in reaction to a report that the French had plans to take control of the area.

Indeed, France had already established a foothold in Texas. In 1686, the explorer La Salle had built Fort St. Louis on the Brazos River. La Salle had landed in Texas accidentally. His ships had sailed into the Gulf of Mexico from France in an attempt to return to the Mississippi River, but they had overshot the entrance to the river. The following year, La Salle abandoned the fort and headed east toward the Mississippi River. Along the way, he was murdered by his own men.

When de León arrived at Fort St. Louis in 1689, he found the skeletons of French settlers who had remained behind when La Salle headed eastward. The following year, de León

OPPOSITE The Apache had dominated Texas in the years before Spanish colonization and proved to be hostile to the Spanish for many years afterward.

built the first mission in Texas, called San Francisco de los Tejas, to begin converting the local Indians to Christianity. Unfortunately, the Spanish brought diseases that killed the Indians by the hundreds. As a result, the mission was unsuccessful in making conversions, and it was soon abandoned.

American Indians in Texas

What the Spanish had not realized was that Texas would prove a very hostile place for establishing missions or any other settlements. For centuries before the coming of the Spanish, Texas was dominated by Apache tribes. They had migrated from Canada to Arizona, New Mexico, and Texas. For their livelihood, the Apache depended in large part on the buffalo. Vast herds of buffalo roamed across the Texas plains and much of the West. These animals were hunted by the Apache, who used buffalo meat for food and buffalo hides to make clothing and tepees. The Apache also raided Pueblo villages for other types of food, such as corn, beans, and squash.

During the 16th and 17th centuries, the Apache encountered Spanish explorers led by Coronado. The Spanish introduced the horse to the Apache. Spanish horses were lost by the conquistadores or ran off to the plains, where they were captured by the Apache. In addition, Apache warriors raided Spanish settlements, taking as many horses as possible. Historian T. R. Fehrenbach wrote, "Apache horsemen now could raid fast and far, striking deep into Spanish territory, and then run back to safety on the endless plains before they could be pursued. On one raid alone in the 1650's, Apaches carried off three hundred horses." With horses, the Apache dominated the Texas plains.

The Apache were not the only Indians whose lives were changed by the horse. In 1725, the Comanche rode onto the Texas plains. According to Fehrenbach, "They came like a thunderbolt. . . . Man, woman, and child, they were among the finest horsemen ever known. They were armed with the long Plains lance and bison-hide shield, hard enough to turn a musket ball, and they could fire a shower of arrows with deadly accuracy from the gallop." The Comanche were more powerful than the Apache, who were not united as a single tribe. As a result, the Comanche drove the Apache southward out of the north-central Texas plains during the first half of the 18th century.

> **Fast Fact**
>
> In Texas, Coronado called some of the American Indians he encountered Tejas. This word means "friends" in the language of the Caddo Indians. Gradually, the area became known as Texas.

San Antonio

While the Apache and Comanche were fighting each other, a Spanish expedition appeared in southeast Texas. In 1716, local Spanish officials decided to send settlers to Texas and establish a new settlement at Nacogdoches, opening trade with French Louisiana. Nacogdoches was located east of the Red River, the border of French Louisiana. Over the next three decades, the Spanish carried on a lucrative trade with the French in Louisiana.

In 1718, the Spanish decided to expand their presence in east Texas. This effort was designed to hold the territory

In addition to the combative Apache, the Spanish had to cope with unfriendly Comanche warriors, such as the one shown here.

in case the French in Louisiana ever began to move westward. The Spanish built a presidio, San Antonio de Béxar and a mission, San Antonio de Valero, on the San Antonio River. In addition, they established a series of missions in east Texas, north of the Gulf coast. These missions were expected to convert American Indians in the small tribes living in the area. Most of the Indians, however, contracted diseases that killed large numbers of them, and there were very few conversions. As a result, these missions were abandoned.

San Antonio de Valero continued to operate. According to a Spanish missionary, it was "the best site in the world, with good and abundant irrigation water, rich lands for pasture, plentiful building stone, and excellent timber." A few settlers came north from New Spain to San Antonio, which had a population of about 200 in 1726. However, tension developed between the Franciscan missionaries and the soldiers in the San Antonio presidio. The missionaries referred to the soldiers as "outlaws, and no-goods." The Franciscans also complained about the Indians who worked in the fields at the missions, accusing them of laziness.

Meanwhile, more settlers arrived in San Antonio from the Canary Islands during the 1730s. The Spanish government lured them to the area by giving them land, as well as the title *hidalgo*. This title was considered a mark of distinction in Spain, reserved for people of the upper classes. The hidalgos were not expected to till their own fields in Spain, but hired laborers to do the work for them. The hidalgos in east Texas wanted the American Indians to work their lands. They became upset at the missionaries, because most of the Indians already worked at the missions. In turn, the missionaries accused the hidalgos of being "indolent and given to vice" for not farming the land themselves.

By the 1770s, little improvement had occurred at San Antonio. In 1777, Teodoro de Croix, general of the Interior Provinces, reported that the people of San Antonio "live miserable lives because of their laziness . . . and lack of means of support, all of which defects show themselves at first sight." One resident of the settlement added, "We were of the poor people . . . to be poor in that day meant to be very poor indeed. . . . But we were not dissatisfied. . . . There was time to eat and sleep and watch the plants growing. Of food, we did not have overmuch—beans and chili, chili and beans."

Missions and Presidios

Meanwhile, Franciscan missionaries and Spanish soldiers had been establishing new missions in Texas. The Franciscans built a string of missions along the rivers in eastern Texas during the 1740s. Then they journeyed northward, pushing out the frontiers of Texas and constructing more missions. These included San Francisco Xavier in 1751 and San Sabá in 1757.

The mission and presidio that the Spanish established at San Sabá were located in the heart of Apache country. The Comanche grew angry with the Spanish for showing such an interest in converting the Apache and putting a new mission in the midst of the Apache hunting grounds.

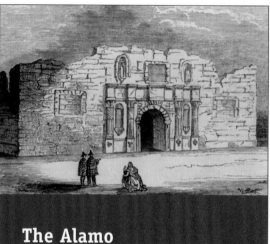

The Alamo

Among the missions taken over by the Spanish government was San Antonio de Valero, which became known as the Alamo. It was turned into a presidio for a garrison of Spanish troops. In 1836, the Alamo was the site of a famous battle in the Texas War of Independence. The independent Republic of Texas was established later that year. Texas joined the United States in 1845.

In March 1758, a large band of 2,000 Comanche swooped down on the presidio and mission at San Sabá. One priest said of the attack that "a furious outburst of yells and war cries was heard outside the gate." The Comanche "were armed with guns and arrayed in the most horrible attire." The Indians easily overwhelmed the Spanish. Priests and soldiers were brutally killed by Indian arrows and lances and then scalped. The mission was completely destroyed, although the San Sabá presidio was strong enough to withstand the attack.

A year later, in 1759, the Spanish launched an expedition against the Comanche. Approximately 360 soldiers marched out of San Antonio under the command of Diego Ortiz Parrilla. Colonel Parrilla was a career officer who had served along the frontier of New Spain. The small army he commanded moved north to San Sabá and then into Comanche territory. There, the troops encountered a large band of Indians, including Comanche and Wichita. Parrilla had brought along two cannons, which he began firing at the Indians. The Indians then charged his small army, driving it back into a wooded area. "The next day," according to historian Randolph Campbell, "Ortíz Parrilla retreated toward San Sabá, having suffered fifty-two casualties, the worst defeat for Spanish arms in Texas."

A New Spanish Policy

By the 1760s, the Spanish recognized that the policy of building presidios and missions was not an effective way to settle Texas. Very few American Indians had been drawn into alliances with the Spanish, and the Comanche in north Texas easily outfought the small garrisons in the presidios.

A government inspection of the northern missions revealed that they had failed to convert many Indians. The presidios were also poorly run. At one presidio, according to the report, "Most of the soldiers were clothed in rags, largely because they could not afford goods sold by the commandant [who received all the supplies from Mexico] who demanded a 1,000 percent profit from his store." The presidios provided very little protection to Spanish settlers.

In 1770, Spain began a new policy called the New Regulations of Presidios. The missions and presidios north of San Antonio were closed and the settlers moved south, around San Antonio, the capital of Spanish Texas.

San Antonio had a presidio and several missions. They included Concepción, San José, and San Juan. The mission at San Juan was a major trading center. Fields were irrigated around the mission, and the American Indians who worked the land grew many fruits and vegetables, including melons, grapes, peaches, and peppers. The mission also raised corn and cattle. Nearby was a new town that had been established at Laredo.

The New Regulations also called for a different policy for dealing with the Indians. By the 1760s, Spain had acquired the colony of Louisiana. The lieutenant governor of Natchitoches on the Red River, Athanase de Meziéres, was an expert in Indian affairs. For many years, the French had created strong alliances with the Indians by trading with them. They had not relied on missions to convert the Indians. De Meziéres, for example, had established good relations with the Wichita, allies of the Comanche. In 1771, de Meziéres managed to sign a peace treaty with the Wichita, removing them as a threat in the central plains of Texas.

The relationship between Louisiana and Texas grew closer during the period of the American Revolution. In 1779, Governor Bernardo de Gálvez of Louisiana traveled to San Antonio to obtain supplies for his troops, whom he planned to lead on a campaign against the British. Cattle ranches had been established in east Texas during the 18th century by the Franciscan missions, well-to-do settlers who had migrated to Texas, and soldiers from the presidios who had acquired land. Gálvez purchased 2,000 head of cattle and took them eastward. The cattle traveled along the Old

San Antonio Road into Natchitoches and central Louisiana. According to historian Randolph Campbell, this was the beginning of the Texas cattle drives that became so common during the next century. About 15,000 head of cattle were driven from Texas into Louisiana between 1779 and 1782.

Communications within the colony of Texas had improved by the 1780s. The Spanish established several post offices which sent letters between Texas and Mexico City. In addition, two roads ran across Texas and connected the colony with Louisiana.

Nevertheless, the threat from the Comanche and Apache had not disappeared. Texas governor Domingo Cabello wrote in 1779, "There is not an instant by day or night when reports do not arrive from all these ranches of barbarities and disorders falling on us. Totally unprotected as we are, they will result in the absolute destruction and loss of this province."

Conditions improved during the 1780s. In 1785, the Spanish authorities sent Pedro Vial, the Frenchman who had opened a route from Arizona and New Mexico to Texas, to parley with the Indians. Vial was well known among the Wichita for his expertise at fixing their guns. He had also traded with the Wichita for many years.

The Wichita chiefs, who had already made peace with the Spanish, agreed to accompany Vial to meet the Comanche. Vial brought lavish presents for the Comanche and promised to bring them valuable trade goods, such as cooking pots and gunpowder. He reminded them that without peace, they would be unable to get these goods.

Vial urged the chiefs to come to San Antonio and make peace with the Spanish.

The Comanche chiefs agreed and rode to San Antonio, where they signed a peace treaty with Governor Cabello. They also agreed to join the Spanish in a war against their enemies, the Apache. As a result, the Apache were defeated in Texas, and conditions along the frontier improved even further.

However, this improvement did not occur in time to persuade the Franciscans to remain in Texas. By this time, they had grown weary of trying to make converts among the Indians. The Franciscans planned to leave the area and concentrate their efforts in other parts of the Spanish Empire. As a result, the Texas missions were gradually taken over by the Spanish government.

A New Threat to the Spanish in Texas

While the Spanish were dealing with one problem, another one arose. After the end of the American Revolution, U.S. settlers began a large migration westward over the Appalachian Mountains. While Texas had a small population of just over 3,000 settlers in 1790, the United States had 277, 000 people living west of the Appalachians. U.S. citizens had already been invited to live in Louisiana.

Texas was a different situation. This area was located on the northern border of New Spain. Spanish officials were afraid that new immigrants would overwhelm the existing settlements. In addition, they feared that U.S. traders might try to establish relations with the American Indian tribes and turn them away from Spain. Texas governor Manuel Muñoz was ordered to take "the utmost care to prevent the passage to this kingdom of persons from the United States of America. The king has been informed on good authority that the United States has ordered emissaries to move here and work to subvert the population."

Nevertheless, the Spanish were unable to completely close the border to these "emissaries." Among them was Philip Nolan, the first filibuster in Texas. Nolan worked for General James Wilkinson, head of the Kentucky militia. Wilkinson had gone to New Orleans in the 1780s and met the Spanish governor, Esteban Miró. In 1791, Governor Miró gave Nolan permission to travel to Texas on a trading expedition. He eventually brought back 50 wild horses for sale in Louisiana. Nolan made two more expeditions during the late 1790s, bringing 1,200 more horses out of Texas.

By this time, the authorities in Texas were becoming suspicious of Nolan and feared that he might be a U.S. spy. When he returned to Texas again in 1800, the Spanish were ready for him. His camp was attacked by troops from Nacogdoches. "As day broke," one of Nolan's men later wrote, "without speaking a word, they commenced their fire. After about ten minutes, our gallant leader Nolan was slain by a musket-ball which hit him in the head."

Three years later, the United States acquired Louisiana. President Thomas Jefferson believed that the Louisiana

> **Fast Fact**
>
> *Filibuster* was a term used by the Spanish, from the word *filibustero*, to describe someone who defied the authorities. Today, the term is used to describe an effort, especially by U.S. senators, to defy the majority and delay the passage of a bill by making lengthy speeches.

Looking for Lewis and Clark

In 1804, President Thomas Jefferson sent an expedition led by Meriwether Lewis and William Clark to explore the lands of the Louisiana Purchase. When the Spanish authorities in the Southwest heard of this, officials in New Mexico sent out several expeditions from Santa Fe to try to head off Lewis and Clark. None of these expeditions, led by Pedro Vial and José Jarvet, located the U.S. explorers. Finally, in 1806, a fourth expedition left Santa Fe, led by Lieutenant Facundo Melgares. He reached present-day Nebraska before turning back. Meanwhile, Lewis and Clark were returning from their journey less than 200 miles (321 km) away, along the Missouri River.

Purchase also included Texas and all the land northward. The Spanish, of course, disagreed. By 1806, the Spanish had sent more troops to the area around Nacogdoches to prevent what they feared might be a U.S. invasion. War was finally avoided when both countries agreed to establish a neutral ground between Louisiana and Texas. This was a strip of land between the Red River and the Sabine River, just east of Nacogdoches.

Zebulon Pike

This was not the last problem that arose between the United States and Spain. During the negotiations over the neutral ground, the U.S. government was sending explorers into the area newly acquired from France. The Lewis and Clark expedition traveled into the lands of the Louisiana Purchase in 1804. In 1805, Lieutenant Zebulon Pike headed west from St. Louis with a small expedition to explore the new territory.

Pike later claimed that he got lost and wandered into Spanish New

Mexico. On March 3, 1806, after traveling through frigid weather, Pike and his men arrived in Santa Fe. He said that the town "struck my mind with the same effect as a fleet of flat bottomed boats, which are seen in the spring and fall seasons, descending the Ohio River. There are two churches, the magnificence of whose steeples form a striking contrast to the miserable appearance of the houses."

The Spanish did not want a U.S. explorer in New Spain. Pike was eventually sent back to New Orleans by way of San Antonio, accompanied by Spanish troops. According to historian T. R. Fehrenbach,

> *Pike kept a clear, trained eye on his travels through New Mexico, Texas, and New Spain. [He] . . . was astounded at the luxury of Spanish officialdom— Spanish officers traveled about with burros loaded with delicacies and wines. But he also saw and reported the rags and indiscipline of the common soldiery. . . . If it came to war, this country was ripe for plucking, or so many Americans thought.*

Soon the Spanish government that ran the country would be replaced by an independent Mexico.

The Mexican Revolution

6

By the early 19th century, the Spanish had been ruling New Spain for almost three centuries. Their vast empire stretched from the North American Southwest across Central America and into South America. Much of the population of New Spain, approximately 6 million people, lived in small villages and towns spread across the entire empire. Many others were concentrated in major cities like Guadalajara, Vallodolid, and the capital, Mexico City.

The capital was a magnificent city with spacious squares, sumptuous buildings, and ornate homes for the wealthy, who dressed in the latest European fashions. Members of the upper class held expensive parties for their friends, read the latest books, and had their portraits painted by local artists. The carriages of the well-to-do crammed the city streets, which were illuminated at night with street lighting.

Most of the wealthy settlers were Spaniards. A small number of them, about 15,000, were known as *gachupines,* because they had been born in Spain. The other Spaniards—

OPPOSITE This hand-colored woodcut shows members of New Spain's upper class outside the palace of Mexico City in the 1800s.

over 900,000—were known as *criollos,* or creoles. They were born in New Spain, although their ancestors were Spanish. Both the gachupines and the criollos were white-skinned.

The Spanish king appointed gachupines to almost all the major positions in the colonial government, believing that they had the strongest loyalty to Spain. Almost all the 170 viceroys in the history of New Spain were gachupines, as were most of the 602 commanding generals of the Spanish army garrisoned there. In addition, the overwhelming majority of the 706 bishops who led the Catholic Church in New Spain were gachupines.

The criollos felt excluded from power in New Spain because they could fill only lesser positions. Some were local government employees, while others were lawyers, doctors, craftspeople, small business owners, and Catholic priests. A few criollos became wealthy silver mine owners and ranchers. However, the gachupines formed the upper class, or aristocracy, of New Spain, holding most of the power and wealth. Most criollos were members of the middle class.

The vast majority of the people in the empire were poor. They included American Indians; mestizos, who were of mixed Indian and Spanish ancestry; African-American slaves, who worked on the large ranchos and plantations; and castes, who were people of mixed Indian, Spanish, and African ancestry. By the early 19th century, according to historian Hugh Hamill, "the Spaniards were generally hated by the American criollos and the lower classes."

Nevertheless, these classes were not united. The criollos regarded themselves as being far above the lower classes. They wanted to share power with the gachupines. As one

observer put it, "In America, the skin, more or less white, is what dictates the class that an individual occupies in society. A white, even if he rides barefoot on horseback, considers himself a member of the nobility of the country."

The lower classes in New Spain, such as these Mexican women shown making tortillas, were looked upon with disdain by the upper class.

The Impact of Events in Europe

In 1789, the French Revolution broke out, eventually overthrowing the king and the aristocracy in France. The gachupines feared that a similar rebellion might occur in New Spain. In fact, plots among the criollos to overthrow the government had been discovered in New Spain during the 1790s and stopped before they could cause a revolution.

Miguel Hidalgo y Costilla

Miguel Hidalgo y Costilla (1753–1811), a criollo, was born in 1753 near Guanajuato. His father, Cristóbal was the overseer of a large hacienda, or farm, owned by a wealthy Spaniard. Cristóbal Hidalgo could afford to send his son to school in Valladolid. Miguel attended the College of San Nicolás Obispo, a secondary school that prepared him for college. In 1774, he graduated from the University of Mexico in Mexico City. Four years later, Hidalgo became a priest.

Hidalgo taught at the College of San Nicolás Obispo for more than 15 years. Eventually, he was appointed head of the school. In 1792, he abruptly left the college, although historians are uncertain of the reasons for his decision. That same year, he became a parish priest at a church in Colima, west of Mexico City. From there, he went to another church in San Felipe, and finally, he was appointed to a church in Dolores in 1803.

Meanwhile, French troops under the leadership of Napoleon were spreading across Europe. Napoleon's forces conquered large parts of Europe, overthrowing aristocratic governments and putting French officials in charge. In 1808, French armies invaded Spain and drove out King Ferdinand VII.

In New Spain, the upper classes felt that they owed no loyalty to a French king. Instead, the Spanish planned to set up a new government that would rule New Spain until Ferdinand VII could regain his power. In Mexico City, a group of criollos took power, with the assistance of the Spanish viceroy, José de Iturrigaray. He believed that the future of New Spain lay with the criollos. The gachupines, who controlled the army, were horrified. Iturrigaray was driven out of Mexico City, and the rebel criollos were arrested.

Revolution had been avoided, but only for the time being. A plot was uncovered in Vallodolid in 1809 and stopped by the Spanish government. Then, a year later, another uprising broke out that could not be stopped.

The Hidalgo Revolt

The revolt that eventually led to independence began in Dolores, a small town located north of Mexico City. The leader of the revolt was a Catholic priest, Miguel Hidalgo y Costilla. Dolores was a poor community, with many Indians and mestizos. When Hidalgo arrived there in 1803, he began programs designed to provide jobs for the poor.

Criollos gathered at Hidalgo's house to discuss the latest events in Europe and the political situation in New Spain. As he both recognized the plight of the poor and sympathized with the position of the criollos, Father Hidalgo became the center of a movement to change the government of New Spain. Along with other criollos, including a cavalry captain named Ignacio Allende, he planned a revolution. The uprising was scheduled to begin on December 8, 1810.

However, word of the uprising was leaked to the Spanish authorities. Hidalgo insisted that the revolutionaries go ahead, earlier than planned. According to one eyewitness, he told them, "Gentlemen, we are lost, there is no recourse but to go and seize gachupines."

With men from Dolores and a few soldiers who supported him, Hidalgo began the revolt. On September 16, 1810, Hidalgo addressed the people of Dolores. In his famous *Grito* [Cry] *de Dolores,* he told them, "The moment of our freedom has arrived; the hour of our liberty has struck; and if you recognized its great value, you will help me defend it from the ambitious grasp of the tyrants." In Dolores, his army captured the local gachupines and put them in prison.

From Dolores, Hidalgo began to lead his small army to other towns. Along the way, the size of the rebel force grew much larger. The army headed southward to the nearby town of San Miguel, Allende's village. Once again, gachupines were arrested and clapped into prison, and a criollo cabildo was established.

The army, now 25,000 strong, headed south to Guanajuato. Many American Indians and mestizos joined the rebels, along with criollos. A pitched battle occurred at Guanajuato as the residents tried to defend themselves. The rebel soldiers finally overran the town's defenders and began to massacre them. Hidalgo could not control the soldiers in his own army, who took out their anger on anyone who opposed them. From Guanajuato, the army, now 60,000 soldiers, reached Vallodolid, which surrendered to Father Hidalgo. His next target was Mexico City.

A lot of the criollos in Mexico City and elsewhere in New Spain were frightened of the rebel movement. Many well-to-do criollos feared that they might suffer the same fate as the gachupines in the small towns that had been invaded by Hidalgo's army. In addition, many poor people failed to join the revolution. Hugh Hamill writes that the criollos who were Catholic priests and town officials "exerted profound influence on the masses not to join Hidalgo." As the priest in one parish put it, the people were "overcome by terror and dread [of Hidalgo's horde] . . . they remain quietly in their homes and wretched huts, so deeply moved are they by my continuous and effective exhortations."

By the time Hidalgo's army reached the outskirts of Mexico City, it was running short of ammunition.

Nevertheless, it defeated a Spanish army on October 30. Afterward, Hidalgo decided that this army was too weak to overcome the Spanish defenders within the capital. Support from criollos inside the capital had also failed to appear. On November 3, Father Hidalgo decided to withdraw.

Hidalgo's troops retreated and entered Valladolid, where they executed 60 gachupines. From there, the army continued northwestward to Guadalajara, where more executions occurred. On January 11, 1811, Hidalgo's army met Spanish troops on the battlefield at the Bridge of Calderón. A wagon carrying ammunition for Hidalgo's troops was hit by government artillery fire. The wagon exploded, causing Hidalgo's men to panic and flee from the field and giving the Spanish the victory. In March, Hidalgo, Allende, and a few of their men were captured by the government forces. Hidalgo and Allende were then tried and executed.

On its way to Mexico City in 1810, the army of Father Miguel Hidalgo y Costilla battled the gachupines in power in smaller towns, arresting them and replacing them with criollos.

The Aftermath of the Revolt

After the death of Hidalgo, the rebel leadership passed to others, including a priest, José María Morelos, who was a mestizo. He was captured in 1815 and executed. After his death, rebel leaders Guadalupe Victoria and Vicente Guerrero kept small armies operating in the countryside, where the Spanish army was unable to corner them.

In 1820, the government sent one of its generals, Agustín de Iturbide, to meet with Guerrero and try to bring an end to the warfare. Instead, General Iturbide, a criollo, made a deal with the rebel leader. Both of them agreed to support the independence of Mexico. On February 24, 1821, they issued the Plan de Iguala. It included three guarantees. Mexico would become a constitutional monarchy; the Roman Catholic Church would retain all its power over the country's religious life; and criollos and gachupines would have equal power in the new government.

Spain did not immediately recognize the new Plan de Iguala. Later in the year, however, the Spanish government realized that it did not have the manpower to take back control of Mexico. The Spanish government signed an agreement with Iturbide recognizing Mexican independence.

The Iturbide Government

Iturbide selected a new group of administrators to govern Mexico—mainly criollos. However, the Mexican congress, which was part of the new government, wanted to reduce the size of Iturbide's army. Fearing that his own future might be in jeopardy, Iturbide decided to change the government. With the help of his soldiers, he declared himself Emperor Agustín I in 1822, establishing the Mexican Empire.

As a result of the long civil war, the economy of Mexico had been hurt. Mining operations at the rich silver mines had been reduced, and farmland had been destroyed. Iturbide had no solutions for these problems.

Fast Fact

While Mexico was achieving its independence, similar movements were under way throughout the Spanish empire in South America. These efforts were led by Simón Bolívar and José Francisco de San Martin. By the early 1820s, all the Spanish colonies on the continent had become independent.

Mexicans rapidly began blaming the emperor for their economic difficulties. He jailed some of his critics, and many Mexicans accused him of being a tyrant. They began to plan a rebellion to overthrow the emperor. Among the leaders of the revolt was Antonio López de Santa Anna, a general at Veracruz, on the Mexican coast. He was supported by Vicente Guerrero. Emperor Agustín sent an army under the command of José Antonio Echáverri to deal with Santa Anna. Instead, the two men made a deal to combine their armies and drove Iturbide off the throne.

Thus the empire came to an end, and an independent republic was declared in Mexico City in 1823. The political changes occurring in Mexico had a major impact on California and the Southwest.

The Revolution on the Frontier

7

I n December 1808, Texas settlers held a five-day festival in honor of the Immaculate Conception and Virgin of Guadalupe. They danced and sang and held bullfights. The festivities were interrupted by a proclamation from the governor, Manuel de Salcedo:

> *The desire I have to contribute to the satisfaction of the settlers cannot be the cause of my neglecting my sacred obligation to preserve the province from the fatal destruction of the revolution which has engulfed certain settlements in the viceroyalty. It may be justly feared that the revolutionary leaders may have some partisans here.*

In fact, a revolution was already brewing in Texas. Led by a soldier named Juan Bautista de las Casas, settlers unhappy with Spanish rule were planning to overthrow the governor. In January 1811, they struck. Salcedo and his men were thrown into jail and later escorted out of Texas. Las

OPPOSITE In 1808, at a Texas festival in honor of the Virgin of Guadalupe, shown here, Spanish governor Manuel de Salcedo expressed his hope that he could keep revolution against Spanish rule from coming to Texas.

Casas became the head of a new government in Texas. Soon after the revolt in Texas, however, Father Hidalgo was defeated at the Battle of Calderón. Las Casas, who was not well liked by Texas settlers, was himself overthrown and replaced by a royalist government. Word of his overthrow reached Salcedo's captors, who freed the governor. In fact, they helped capture Father Hidalgo, who was fleeing northward after his defeat at Calderón.

Soon afterward, Salcedo returned to San Antonio and resumed his duties as governor of Texas. Although Father Hidalgo had been executed, the revolution continued in Mexico. Revolutionaries tried to gather support from the United States. In 1811, Bernardo Gutiérrez traveled to Washington, D.C., to meet with U.S. president James Madison. Madison did not provide any aid to the Mexican revolutionaries, so Gutiérrez decided to take matters into his own hands.

Operating out of Natchitoches, he built a small army that included many U.S. citizens who sympathized with Mexican independence. Calling themselves the Republican Army of the North, they marched into Texas in 1812. In August, the army took control of Nacogdoches, across the Texas border, and marched on Goliad. Gutiérrez announced to the Texas settlers, "Rise en masse, soldiers and citizens; unite in the holy cause of our country! I am now marching to your succor with a respectable force of American volunteers who have left their homes and families to take up our cause, to fight for our liberty."

After capturing Goliad, Gutiérrez and his army were confronted by Governor Salcedo, who had marched out from San Antonio. Salcedo's army laid siege to Goliad in 1812 but was unable to capture it and finally retreated. The Army of the North then advanced toward San Antonio, defeating Salcedo's army several miles outside the Texas capital. Salcedo and other officials in his government were tried and sentenced to death. Then the U.S. citizens in Gutiérrez's army insisted that the lives of the governor and his supporters should be spared. Salcedo and the others were removed from the courtroom and supposedly taken to jail. Along the way, they were murdered.

Gutiérrez, who called himself the president protector of Texas, was not well liked by the men in his army. By early August 1813, he had been overthrown and replaced by José Alvarez de Toledo. Meanwhile, an army of 2,000 Spanish royalists was heading toward San Antonio under the command of Colonel Joaquín Arredondo.

A four-hour battle was fought outside the capital on August 18. Arredondo reported that those in the rebel army "found themselves confronted by the main body of our army formed in line for attack, with artillery placed on the flanks of our cavalry." The Army of the North was defeated, and Arredondo rounded up its leaders. Many of them, along with their families, were thrown into prison. More than 300 soldiers were executed.

As head of the army, Arredondo now took control of the colony. Hundreds of settlers fled from Texas rather than live under Arredondo's rule. The population of 4,000 was reduced by as much as one-half. One observer noted that the situation was reduced to "chaos and misery" as Arredondo and his men "drained the resources of the country, and laid their hands on everything that could sustain human life." Historian W. D. C. Hall added, "Texas was essentially reduced to its pre-Spanish mission wilderness state."

Meanwhile, Spain and the United States finally agreed on the boundary line between Louisiana and Texas. According to the Adams-Onis Treaty of 1819, the line ran along the Sabine River. Nevertheless, the treaty did not end the threats to Spanish control of Texas. As U.S. citizens pushed westward, they hoped to add Texas to the United States. U.S. settlements had already sprung up on Galveston Island, off the coast of southern Texas. Galveston was also the headquarters of a pirate named Jean Lafitte. Under his command were as many as 20 ships that preyed on Spanish commerce along the Texas coast.

This colored engraving from 1844 shows pirate Jean Lafitte and his men capturing a Spanish merchant ship. Lafitte's base was the island of Galveston, off the Texas coast.

Galveston Island was home to other buccaneers as well. They included José Manuel Herrera and Louis Michel Aury, who wanted Galveston to become part of the Mexican Republic. Among their associates was Henry Perry, who had been part of the Republican Army of the North. Perry had led an invasion of Spanish Texas in 1817, but he had been defeated at the Battle of Perdido, near Goliad, by Governor Antonio Martinez.

Two years later, after the Adams-Onis Treaty had been signed, another invasion occurred. It was led by Colonel James Long, a merchant from Natchez, Louisiana. Long raised an army of about 300 filibusters. He tried to gather additional support from Lafitte, but the pirate turned him down. Nevertheless, in 1819, Long invaded Texas with his small army and took control of Nacogdoches. A short time later, he was driven out of Texas by Spanish troops. In 1821, Long invaded Texas again. This time, he was captured, and he later died in prison in Mexico City.

Jane Long

Jane Long (1798–1880) was the niece of General James Wilkinson. She had accompanied her husband, James, during his first invasion of Texas in 1819. When James Long invaded for a second time in 1821, he left his wife at Point Bolivar, in present-day Texas. She was accompanied by the families of other men who had joined Long's army. These families eventually returned to the United States, but Jane Long remained at Point Bolivar. In 1821, her daughter Mary Long was born. She is considered the first Anglo-American child born in Texas.

New Mexico and Arizona

While Spanish officials were dealing with Long, Mexican independence had been declared by General Iturbide in Mexico City. By September, Governor Facundo Melgares in

Santa Fe had received word of independence. In December, the Iturbide government directed Melgares to hold a public ceremony marking independence.

The ceremony occurred on January 6, 1822. Governor Melgares announced that the settlers should "make the tyrants see that . . . at the cost of our last drop of blood we will sustain the sacred independence of the Mexican Empire." The celebration included a parade in the town square, cannon fire, and a fancy dress ball at the governor's home that continued until 4:30 the following morning.

Mexican independence brought an end to the trade restrictions between Mexico and the United States that had been enforced under the Spanish. U.S. traders regarded New Mexico, as well as Arizona, as lucrative areas for doing business. They hoped to trade for fur pelts captured by Spanish trappers. In addition, U.S. traders were aware of the silver mines in the Southwest and hoped to exchange their goods for Spanish silver.

Late in 1821, the first expedition of U.S. traders, led by William Becknell, arrived in Santa Fe from Missouri. Becknell brought only a small quantity of goods, but he rapidly sold all of them in Santa Fe. In 1822, he came back to Santa Fe, leading wagons loaded with trade items. This was the beginning of the trade that operated along the Santa Fe Trail from Missouri to the Southwest. U.S. citizens, as well as Mexican merchants, participated in the trade, which grew stronger and stronger over the next 25 years. In fact, the Santa Fe Trail became one of the most famous routes for travel from the United States to New Mexico.

A wagon train is shown arriving in Santa Fe, New Mexico, in this engraving from around 1840.

California

Other traders carried goods to Arizona and as far west as California. Here, they traded for hides of animals that were raised at Spanish missions and large ranchos. In California, Spanish citizens had developed huge ranchos where they raised cattle. Cattle hides were highly prized because they could be made into leather for clothing and shoes. U.S. ships from the eastern seaboard sailed around the tip of South America and into California ports to buy these hides, as well as large quantities of sea otter furs. California was part of a worldwide trade that took U.S. merchant

An Early San Francisco Love Story

Although the Spanish tried to keep other trappers out of San Francisco, U.S. and Russian ships regularly sailed there to participate in the fur trade. In 1805, a Russian ship sailed into San Francisco Bay to trade. Among the passengers on board the ship was Nikolai Rezanov, a member of the court of Czar Alexander I, ruler of Russia.

While staying in San Francisco, Rezanov met Concepcion Arguello, the daughter of the Spanish governor. In a short time, the couple became engaged. However, Rezanov had not completed his mission, and he asked his fiancée to postpone their marriage until he could come back from Russia for her. Unfortunately, Rezanov did not return, because he died in Russian Siberia. Concepcion waited for him for 10 years, until she finally learned of his death. Eventually, she became a nun until her own death in 1857.

ships east to China. In China, they sold furs and purchased spices and tea to be sold in California on the return trip westward.

California in the early 19th century was largely cut off from the rest of the world, except for the visits of a few merchant ships. As a result, events in Mexico were slow to become known to the Californios. While the revolution was under way, little news of it ever reached California, which remained strongly royalist.

Finally, in 1818, news reached California that the colony might be attacked by a pirate ship. Aboard the ship, commanded by Hippolyte de Bouchard, were many U.S. citizens who supported the independence movement in Mexico. Late in the year, de Bouchard arrived at Monterey with two ships. When he asked the Spanish to sell him supplies, they turned him down. Firing broke out between the presidio at Monterey and de Bouchard's ships. Fearing he was greatly outnumbered, Governor Pablo de Sola retreated from Monterey. De Bouchard occupied the port, burned it, and then sailed away in his ships. Although he was expected to strike San Diego in 1819, de Bouchard never appeared. Instead, he left for Chile and Peru, where he participated in the wars of independence in South America.

By 1821, Mexico had become independent, but the news did not reach California until the following year. On April 11, 1822, Governor de Sola ordered that California should become part of independent Mexico. To the accompaniment of music and fireworks, California raised the Mexican flag over Monterey.

The Mexican Empire, including California, New Mexico, Arizona, and Texas, faced serious problems over the next few decades. Chief among them was the continuing pressure from the westward migration of U.S. settlers. Because of the small Spanish-American population in the areas controlled by Mexico, Mexican authorities would be forced to consider allowing U.S. citizens to establish new settlements inside the Mexican Empire. These settlements eventually led to friction between the Mexican authorities and the U.S. settlers, finally bringing about the Mexican-American War (1846–1848). As a result of the Mexican defeat in the war, the culture of the Southwest and the lives of the Mexican Americans who lived there would change forever. ▣

> **Fast Fact**
>
> The Spanish introduced many new words to their English-speaking neighbors as they settled in the Southwest. *Canyon, plaza, mesa,* and *tortilla* all have their origins in the Spanish language.

Timeline

1610	The Spanish establish a settlement at Santa Fe, New Mexico.
1680	The Pueblo Indians revolt in New Mexico and Arizona.
1690s	The Spanish recover New Mexico.
1700	Father Eusebio Kino establishes the first mission in Arizona.
1706	The Spanish found Albuquerque, New Mexico.
1718	The Spanish establish a settlement at San Antonio, Texas.
1751	The Pima Indians revolt in Arizona.
1752	The Spanish establish a presidio in Tubac, Arizona.
1762	Louisiana becomes part of the Spanish Empire.
1769	A Spanish expedition arrives in Alta California and establishes the first mission at San Diego.
1770	A mission is established at Monterey.
1771	The first settlement is established at Tucson, Arizona.
1776	The Spanish establish a settlement at San Francisco, California.
1782	The Spanish have four presidio districts in California.
1786	The Spanish conclude a peace agreement with the Comanche tribe.
1803	Louisiana becomes part of the United States.
1806	Zebulon Pike arrives in Santa Fe.
1810	Father Miguel Hidalgo y Costilla begins the struggle for Mexican independence.
1811	Hidalgo is executed by the Spanish.
1821	Agustín de Iturbide establishes independent Mexico; California, Texas, New Mexico, and Arizona become part of Mexico.

Glossary

alcalde A town official.

cabildo A form of Spanish city government.

Californios Spanish settlers of California.

criollos Settlers born in Latin America to Spanish parents.

encomienda A system under which American Indians granted their labor to the Spanish and paid them tribute, in return for which the Spanish were responsible for protecting and converting the Indians.

filibuster An adventurer from the United States who invaded or tried to start revolutions in Latin American countries in the late 1700s and 1800s.

gachupines Settlers in New Spain who were born in Spain.

hidalgo A Spanish knight or nobleman.

kachinas Divine spirits of dead Pueblo Indians.

kivas Underground rooms built by Pueblos for holding their ceremonies.

mestizo A person with both Spanish and American Indian ancestry.

New Spain Mexico, the present-day U.S. Southwest, and Central America.

presidio A fort and garrison.

pueblo A town.

regidores Members of a cabildo.

repartimiento A law requiring American Indians to work Spanish lands; the Indians were supposed to be paid but often were not.

shaman An American Indian medicine man.

viceroy The governor of New Spain.

Further Reading

Books

Campbell, Randolph. *Gone to Texas*. New York: Oxford University Press, 2003.

Din, Gilbert C. and Harkins, John. *The New Orleans Cabildo*. Baton Rouge: Louisiana State University Press, 1996.

Hall, Gwendolyn. *Africans in Colonial Louisiana*. Baton Rouge: Louisiana State University Press, 1996.

Kessell, John. *Spain in the Southwest*. Norman, OK: University of Oklahoma Press, 2002.

Meyer, Michael C., et al. *The Course of Mexican History*. New York: Oxford University Press, 1999.

Wagoner, Jay. *Early Arizona*. Tucson: University of Arizona Press,1989.

Web Sites

Colonial Life in Spanish California during the North American Revolution, http://www.americanrevolution.org/cal.html

The Handbook of Texas Online, http://www.tsha.utexas.edu/handbook/online/

Lt. Zebulon Pike's Diary: New Mexico, Chihuahua and Texas, http://www.tamu.edu/ccbn/dewitt/pikejour.htm

Ranch and Mission Days in Alta California, http://www.sfmuseum.org/hist2/rancho.html

Bibliography

Books

Cleland, Robert Glass. *From Wilderness to Empire: A History of California.* New York: Knopf, 1959.

Fehrenbach, T. R. *Lone Star.* New York: Macmillan, 1968.

Hamill, Hugh M., Jr. *The Hidalgo Revolt.* Gainesville, FL: University of Florida Press, 1966.

Krell, Dorothy, et al. *The California Missions.* Menlo Park, CA: Lane Publishing Company, 1979.

Moquin, Wayne, ed. *A Documentary History of the Mexican Americans,* New York: Praeger, 1971.

Simmons, Marc. *New Mexico, A History.* New York: Norton, 1977.

Vella, Christina. *Intimate Enemies.* Baton Rouge: Louisiana State University Press, 1997.

Web Sites

AmericanRevolution.org. "'Colonial Life in Spanish California During the North American Revolution." URL: http://www.americanrevolution.org/cal.html. Downloaded on May 2, 2006.

PBS. "New Perspectives on the West: Junipero Serra." URL: http://www.pbs.org/weta/thewest/people/s_z/serra.htm. Downloaded on May 2, 2006.

The Virtual Museum of the City of San Francisco. "Ranch and Mission Days in Alta California." URL: http://www.sfmuseum.org/hist2/rancho.html. Downloaded on May 2, 2006.

Index

About the Author

Richard Worth

Richard Worth holds a B.A. and an M.A. in colonial American history from Trinity College, Connecticut. He currently teaches writing to third and fourth graders. Worth is the author of several books for middle-grade readers and young adults, including *Westward Expansion and Manifest Destiny, American Slave Trade, Plantation Life,* and *Gangs and Crime,* which was included on the New York Public Library's 2003 Best Books for the Teen Age list. He also wrote *Africans in America and Mexican Immigrants* in Facts on File's Immigration to the United States set.

Mark Overmyer-Velázquez

Mark Overmyer-Velázquez, general editor and author of the preface included in each of the volumes, holds a BA in History and German Literature from the University of British Columbia, and MA, MPhil and PhDs in Latin American and Latino History from Yale University. While working on a new book project on the history of Mexican migration to the United States, he teaches undergraduate and graduate courses in Latin American and U.S. Latina/o history at the University of Connecticut.